## YESSS!
## YOU ARE THERE!

—Face to face with snarling superstar Jimmy Connors in a confrontation that shakes the airways.

—Striving to keep your voice steady as the Knicks make their miraculous run for the NBA championship.

—Calling the plays at a pro football game when you have to duck snowballs thrown by the fans.

—Describing the flying puck and flying fists in an out-of-control hockey game.

—Trying without hope of success to keep Casey Stengel's monologues on the track.

—And everywhere else in the wide and sometimes wacky world of sportscasting as one of America's most popular announcers calls them as he sees them.

**It's a winner!**

NBC

# YESSS!

## MARV ALBERT ON SPORTSCASTING

BY MARV ALBERT WITH HAL BOCK

An Associated Features Book

A SIGNET BOOK

**NEW AMERICAN LIBRARY**

TIMES MIRROR

Copyright © 1979 by Associated Features Inc.

SIGNET TRADEMARK REG. U.S. PAT. OFF. AND FOREIGN COUNTRIES
REGISTERED TRADEMARK—MARCA REGISTRADA
HECHO EN CHICAGO, U.S.A.

SIGNET, SIGNET CLASSICS, MENTOR, PLUME and MERIDIAN
BOOKS are published by The New American Library, Inc.,
1301 Avenue of the Americas, New York, New York 10019

First Printing, October, 1979

1 2 3 4 5 6 7 8 9

PRINTED IN THE UNITED STATES OF AMERICA

# CONTENTS

Introduction I by Al Albert   xi

Introduction II by Steve Albert   xiv

1  Yesss! And It Counts!   1

2  Play-by-play in a Brooklyn Basement   11

3  Hello There, Everybody   25

4  The Daily Show   39

5  The Whole World Isn't Watching   49

6  Interviewing Is a Two-Way Street   61

7  "Kick Save, and a Beauty!"   73

8  At Home in Any Sport   83

9  Memorable Games   99

10  Color Men   119

11  Dear Marv   128

12  Putting a Head on the Commercial   137

13  The Fish that Saved Pittsburgh   147

14  The Road to a Job   155

Glossary   168

Appendix   172

# YESSS!

## MARV ALBERT
## ON SPORTSCASTING

Mrs. Albert's Broadcast Team: Al's left, Steve's right.

**To my starting five—**

Benita
Kenny
Jackie
Brian
Denise

# INTRODUCTION BY AL ALBERT

*Marv's brother Al, Voice of the NBA's Denver Nuggets, is a sportscaster on KOA Radio and TV.*

There is one major advantage to growing up with Marv Albert as your older brother and that is you can always testify to the way things really happened. Fact often has a way of squirming out of focus, but I can supply firsthand descriptions of how one of the nation's very best sportscasters got that way. There is, for example, my memory of his earliest play-by-play experience.

Because my brother was not (forgive me, Marv, I cannot tell a lie) what you would call a gifted athlete, he often was relegated to the sidelines during schoolyard games. There, he would join Sam, the ice cream man, who would park his truck just up the street, waiting for the games to end and business to begin. Sam would sit in the cab of his truck and every so often he'd ask Marv for a progress report.

"What inning is it?" Sam would ask. "Top of the fifth, Sam, two out, first and third." After a few weeks, Marv's descriptions became more detailed. Sam would ask his innocent question and Marv would give him the full picture. . . . "Bottom of the seventh . . . man on third . . . one out . . . infield in for a play at the plate . . . they're protecting the one-run lead . . . and the Squirrel's up . . . dangerous man in this spot . . . line drive hitter . . . clutch spot for the Squirrel . . . and he drills one through the hole into left field . . . the run scores, and it's tied at 2-2."

Soon Marv was providing Sam with play-by-play of the entire ball game, regardless of whether Sam asked for it or not. And even after Sam changed his ice cream route, Marv kept on broadcasting. A career had been born.

Then, there was the matter of the development of Marv's trademark, "Yesss!" I was involved firsthand in that one. My brother had set up his own personal press box under one of the playground baskets, complete with a small table, chairs and a pillowcase attached to the fence with his station's call letters WMPA (for Marvin Philip Albert) carefully lettered on it. He even hired me as his statistician and Marv paid well. He promised if I kept the stats for him, he wouldn't pinch me for a week. And he could pinch, so the price was right.

As Marv called the play-by-play, he would always get excited and stand up as the shot neared the rim, obscuring my line of vision to the basket. Each time that happened, I would tug at his pants and ask if the ball went in. If it did, Marv would look back at me, half annoyed at me for breaking his concentration, and answer loudly, "Yesss!" Then I would record the basket on my stat sheet, never realizing for a moment that I was playing a part in broadcasting history. After a while I didn't even have to tug on his pants anymore.

The most memorable moment I've shared with Marv, outside of the Halloween we dropped water balloons from our upstairs window onto unsuspecting trick-or-treaters, was Marv's first New York Knicks broadcast.

It was late one Saturday night when Marv received a call from Marty Glickman, for whom he worked at CBS. Glickman was the Knicks announcer then, but he was stranded in Paris, unable to make plane connections in time for an afternoon game in Boston the next day. So at the age of 20, in January, 1963, Marv Albert was to make his big-league debut.

Taking along his trusty statistician (me), Marv hopped a midnight train out of New York's Grand Central Station. We were delivered to Boston at about 4 A.M., but the excitement curtailed any desire to sleep. Marv bought all the Boston papers, reading everything he could about the game, getting his notes and stat sheet in order. It wasn't many years before that we had sat in front of a television set in our home, turned down the sound of the game, and went to work, Marv announcing play-by-play into a tape recorder and I providing the sound effects and statistics. And now it would be for real. We must have dreamt hard enough.

But Marv almost didn't get to broadcast that first game. The guards at the Boston Garden press gate would not let us in the building. Marv at 20 looked 14 and I appeared much younger than that. They didn't believe Marv was the Knicks announcer for the game and thought we were just two kids trying to crash the gate. The assignment developed so quickly that Marv had no credentials. Desperate, he opened his briefcase and showed the guard nine pounds of preparation for the game. I really don't think the guy believed Marv, but he must have figured if these kids went to such lengths just to get into a ball game, then, what the heck, and he let us pass through the gates.

Marv handled the game beautifully and eventually received more and more work and ultimately became one of the busiest sportscasters in the country.

In this book, he tells how he did it, and how he does it.

# || INTRODUCTION
# || BY STEVE ALBERT

*Marv's youngest brother Steve does play-by-play on radio and television for the New York Mets and the New York Islanders.*

Because I lived in his house I am one of the few people around who knows how Marv Albert developed his play-by-play style. Before he described basketball or football or hockey or any other sport, my brother worked on his technique by broadcasting Ping-Pong.

But that's not so bad because my other brother, Al, and I did the same thing.

Two of us would play Ping-Pong and the third one would do the play-by-play. " . . . Al serves . . . an easy lob . . . Marv returns . . . a smash . . . Al recovers and comes back with a crossing shot . . . Marv hits into the net . . . Al's point . . . "

Does it sound strange? Well our folks thought it was, too. And they wondered when two of us wrestled, imitating "Haystacks" Calhoun and "Killer" Kowalski, while the third one did the broadcast description. And they weren't too sure about our imaginary baseball leagues and all of the other goings-on that we established in the miniature Madison Sqaure Garden-Ebbets Field-Yankee Stadium-Polo Grounds, which existed in our basement.

All of us decided very early in life what we wanted to do. In the fifth grade, I knew I wanted to be a sportscaster. I remember our teacher assigning our class to write a newscast. I was the only one who memorized it. That was the way my brothers did it and that was the way I did it.

I was still in school when Marv began broadcasting Ranger

and Knick games. I remember sitting at home, doing my homework, listening to his play-by-play and thinking of how he was doing what I wanted to be doing some day.

For a person with broadcasting ambitions, growing up with Marv Albert for a brother had an enormous influence. I had a built-in instructor living in my house. Even now, the two opinions I value most are those of my brothers, Marv and Al. Not many people in this business have the advantage I have in being able to turn to them for their opinions.

When Marv and I both showed up on local New York City television stations, working essentially against one another, our folks put a couple of TV sets side-by-side to follow our broadcasts. Our dad enjoys watching sports, but he's not what you'd call a diehard fan. He'll take a transistor radio with an earplug when he goes out, though, just in case the evening is dull. Mom doesn't know a hockey puck from a football, but she made an instant decision on the two hockey leagues. She'd come to Madison Square Garden for NHL Ranger games that Marv was broadcasting and WHA Cleveland Crusader games which I did. She always brought her knitting along and one time she confided to me that she really enjoyed the Crusader games better than the Ranger games.

"Why, Mom?" I wondered, noting that the rest of New York seemed to prefer the NHL to the WHA.

"Because your games are so nice and quiet," she told me.

The WHA, which counted fans, had noticed the same thing.

The genius of any broadcaster is to make even a quiet game exciting and, if you ask me, that is the magic of Marv Albert. Now, through this book, Marv is sharing in the special insights and techniques he brings to broadcasting. It contains the know-how gained from years of experience doing thousands of events. I've listened and learned from him for a long time and now, you can too. The first lesson is simple. Get yourself a Ping-Pong table and try some play-by-play. If you can do that sport, you can do any sport. My brother Marv proved that.

The NewsCenter4 lineup in the mid-70s: seated—left, anchormen Tom Snyder and Chuck Scarborough; standing—Pia Lindstrom, Frank Field, me, Betty Furness, Gene Shalit, and Carl Stokes. (NBC)

# 1 YESSS! AND IT COUNTS

I had just left the NBC Commissary—you know, the one Johnny Carson is always joking about—and was walking down the hall of the seventh floor at the network headquarters. This is where NewsCenter4, NBC's two-hour evening newscast, is put together. It was a few minutes past seven and the show had just gone off the air. I could relax, more or less, for the next couple of hours until the staff got ready for the 11 P.M. edition.

As I turned down the hall I saw Dr. Frank Field, the NBC weatherman, heading toward me. He had just finished his piece on the second hour of the show. As we neared each other Frank broke into a big grin. He stopped dead in his tracks, looked up, as if following the trajectory of a basketball, and then thrust his head down.

"Yesss!" he shouted. I laughed. "Sid Borgia," I thought to myself, "you didn't know what you started."

Sid Borgia was a referee in the National Basketball Association back in the league's early days. He had an emphatic style that added to the color and excitement of pro basketball. He was a distinctive official who'd never be confused with any other ref when he was working. Part of Borgia's routine—for me, the best part—came on a three-point play when the shooter was fouled. Borgia would raise his arm, loading it up as the ball headed for the basket. As it dropped through, Borgia would bring his arm forward to indicate the basket was good, and he'd shout the magic phrase, loud enough for the whole building to hear. "Yesss! And it counts." That meant the basket counted and the shooter was also going to the foul line for a free throw.

During the days when Borgia was the best referee in the NBA,

I was learning my basic basketball on the sidewalks of Brooklyn, N. Y. There is no better classroom than a concrete court in a playground, and that's why they call basketball "The City Game." Kids are showoffs. They like to make believe that they are broadcasting games while they are playing them. There is a certain "high" that a youngster gets when he makes a play and, at the same time, can hear the broadcaster's voice describing it. I was no different. In the playgrounds I was a combination of Marty Glickman, Vin Scully, and Les Keiter—three of New York's more widely heard sportscasters during the days when I was all-schoolyard in my own mind.

A bunch of the same kids would play basketball together in the schoolyard and one of them started incorporating not only the play-by-play broadcast of what was going on, but began using Borgia's emphatic act as well. And that's where I began using the phrase that has become my trademark. "Yesss!" Thank you, Sid Borgia.

"Yesss!" is strictly a basketball term and it obviously doesn't apply for every shot. To qualify for "Yesss," a shot has to be special. Usually, I reserve it for a line drive shot that rattles against the hoop as it goes through. That's a "Yesss!" So is one of Earl Monroe's spinning reverse layups. Anytime a shot brings the fans right out of their seats, that deserves the "Yesss" treatment. To me, the guy who scored the most "Yesss" baskets was Cazzie Russell when he first came into the NBA with the New York Knicks. Russell had a flair for the spectacular, and when he was on the court the sparks really flew.

The first time I ever used "Yesss" was during a playoff game involving the Knicks. Dick Barnett had the ball as time was running out. He was way out, beyond the circle, when he saw only a second or two left on the clock. He just threw the ball up in one of the most farfetched hook shots I've ever seen. Somehow the trajectory was just right, and it banked in off the backboard as the buzzer went off. That was the first "Yesss!" and it earned the honor.

Now, I try to reserve "Yesss!" for really deserving plays. You can tell how good a game is by the number of times I use it. The more "Yesss!" baskets you hear, the better the game I'm broadcasting.

Perhaps, because I grew up in the city playing basketball and because it was the first big-league sport for which I did play-by-play, I feel a special affinity for it. I've always felt something special about broadcasting basketball, especially on radio. That's because in a radio broadcast of a basketball game the announcer is everything. He is the eyes and ears of his audience, which must depend on him totally to know what's going on. And, because of the geography of the court, the game can be captured so well. Frontcourt, backcourt, left corner, right corner, circle, key, or lane. Those are all places on the court, part of the map the broadcaster uses to describe the location of the ball.

With basketball, I feel the most important quality for a broadcaster to have is consistency. The listeners get to recognize a consistency of the call, and they can follow the game because they know the geography.

The professional game of basketball has changed since I started broadcasting. The running style of the pros has created a faster pace for the broadcaster. I used to be able to relax between baskets. But no more. Now almost every team applies pressure in the backcourt, and the ball often changes hands instantly. The announcer must be alert to this in today's game. Scouts look for players with what they call "good court vision." Announcers must have the same quality. Sometimes you can almost anticipate a steal. It's a feel of the flow of the game. When the momentum of a game shifts from one team to the other, the fans know it and so does the broadcaster.

I make it a practice of giving the score of the game after each and every basket, especially on radio. On television the director will sometimes use an inset view of the scoreboard, but on radio, the listener has nothing to look at but that grille-covered speaker, and I have to let him know what the progress of the game is—who's ahead and how much time is left to play. Some people have suggested that repeating the score after every basket is too much, but I don't think so. To me it seems to blend in and is not distracting at all. In fact, when I'm listening to a game instead of broadcasting it, that's something I want to hear from the announcer. When I don't, I feel deprived and that's something I never want my listeners to feel.

The difference between broadcasting a basketball game on radio and doing it on television is like the difference between night and day. On television, the broadcaster must make a conscious effort to shut up and not say the obvious. I believe in saying much less when I'm doing basketball on television. The audience doesn't need a play-by-play man on television to the extent it does on radio.

My television broadcasts are like an edited version of radio play-by-play. I call it economizing. There is no necessity for detailing every pass and mentioning every player who touches the ball on TV. It's there for the viewer to see. On radio, though, I feel an obligation to follow the progress of the ball from player to player. Here is a sequence from a Knicks–Celtics game, first the radio version and then the way the same play would be described on television.

. . . *Score, Celtics 41, Knicks 39. Frazier out of the backcourt, across the midcourt line. Moves to the right side. Holds up. Throws to the head of the foul circle to McAdoo. McAdoo down low to Monroe. Spins along the baseline. Twisting, reverse layup—good!*

. . . *Score, Celtics 41, Knicks 39. Frazier brings it up. McAdoo. Looking for Monroe at the baseline. Beautiful reverse drive.*

The geography on television isn't as necessary as it is on radio because, after all, the viewer can see where the ball is going. The radio listener, of course, cannot. That's why there is less pressure for the play-by-play man on television. On television I'll skip passes all of the time. Often, the color man is still talking about the previous basket as the ball is being brought up court. Or sometimes, the director orders a replay of the last sequence, and the fan at home will be hearing our comments on that while the ball is moving back in play. When that happens we use the catch phrase, "Back live," to indicate the switch from taped action to live action.

You hate to see it happen, but sometimes because of a replay, you'll even miss a basket. That's a little embarrassing, but there's not much you can do except say " . . . while we were away, Jones hit a 20-foot jump shot." In that situation, since the audience had not seen the play, I would describe the basket as specifically as I would in a radio broadcast.

The replay is a marvelous tool, but it can be overused. When to employ it is the decision of the director who works in the remote truck, usually outside of the arena with the producer, sound man, and other technicians. Some directors insist on showing too many baskets and too many fouls on the replay. That's really unnecessary, and I think it can disrupt the flow of the broadcast. And flow is very important to a successful show.

The producer is in charge of the total package, and he's the one who is hooked up to the ear of the announcer through that plug-in device you see us wearing. Let me tell you, it can be kind of distracting to be talking about one subject and have the producer speaking into your ear about something entirely different. A good producer uses the earpiece wisely. The producer also is in constant contact with the stage manager, who sits at courtside with the play-by-play and color men. His job is to see that everything in the arena goes smoothly for us during the show. He is the long arm of the producer.

The stage manager is responsible for the physical arrangement at courtside, including placement of the monitor. Some people believe you should broadcast from that monitor. Marty Glickman, who taught me a lot about this business, is one. The philosophy is that you are seeing exactly what's being seen at home, and, therefore, you should not talk about anything that is not seen on the monitor. I find that difficult. I can't pick out the players as well from that screen. So I find myself shifting back and forth. And anytime it's important for me to know what's being shown on the screen, the producer will tell me through our communications link. He might point out that the camera is showing the coach on the bench or somebody in the crowd. "Look at your monitor," he'll say. Or "Talk about Digger [Phelps]. We're showing him." A good producer, though, won't talk to me that much. Only where it's necessary. Constant chatter distracts.

Sometimes you see two players on a basketball team who just seem to fit together perfectly. They anticipate each other beautifully and watching them work together is like poetry. That's exactly the kind of a feeling a producer likes to have between his play-by-play man and his color commentator. They must mesh together the same way those two basketball players do.

The play-by-play and color men must be careful not to step on one another's lines. Usually, the play-by-play announcer will nod to his partner when he wants the color man to come in. When you work with someone for a while you get a feel for it. There is a certain chemistry that develops.

On radio, the broadcast is nearly all play-by-play when the game is going on. The color comments must be very concise because the ball comes out of the backcourt so fast. If the color man is making a comment and the radio audience can hear the crowd screaming in the background, it sounds like we've missed something. Sometimes that crowd roar will be over something insignificant, but the radio audience doesn't know that. The listeners want to know what's going on while it's going on.

With the Knicks, my partner is Richie Guerin, a longtime NBA star and coach who is a student of the game of basketball. We've worked out a system whereby I'll look for him on free throw situations because that's a natural break. In the NBA, you have a little time because every free-throw situation is two shots. Timeouts are usually reserved for commercials, but we almost always have 10 or 15 seconds between the time the commercial ends and the time the players return to the court. That's on a 60-second commercial. If we're running a 30-second spot, that gives us maybe 45 seconds to go back and forth. Richie knows he will come in following the commercial, and he's prepared to do it. Then, at the end of the game, if we've used up all our commercials, it gives Richie time to set strategy for the final couple of minutes.

The role of the basketball color man is more emphasized on television. He has more time to talk because the camera can show the progress of the ball downcourt and the play-by-play man's description isn't that vital. There is also more room for analysis in college basketball than there is in the pro game. Pro basketball has outlawed the zone defense, but the colleges can still use it or any number of variations off it. That makes college basketball almost a chess game for the two coaches, and the color commentator can play off that for his analysis. On the college games I do for the NBC-TV network, the color man is R. C. "Bucky" Waters, who coached college basketball at West Virginia and Duke and knows the game inside and out and can relate the technical aspects in layman's language.

One of the important differences between broadcasting basketball, or any other sport for that matter, over radio and over television, is the pregame preparation. On radio I can show up perhaps a half hour before the game and chat just briefly with my color man before we go on the air. On television there's a production meeting a couple of hours ahead of time and even a rehearsal before we go live. Basketball is such an impromptu game that the report of the action comes almost automatically. And, on radio, reporting what's going on takes up most of the broadcast time. But on television there are other concerns such as camera placement and the like, so more preparation time is needed.

At our production meetings the play-by-play announcer and color man sit with the stage manager, director, and producer. The producer runs the meeting. Before we sit down he has typed a "show routine," running through each segment of the telecast with time allotment, commercial position and such, carefully outlined. We each have a copy of this "routine" and the producer runs through it with us so that we know the flow of the program. In that way, when we go on the air, there are no surprises.

There are so many things to go over. For example, the producer will remind the stage manager to instruct both teams to have the players take off their warmup jackets as soon as they hit the court. That gives us extra time to identify the players by uniform number and become familiar with them. Remember, college players are less widely known than the pros.

I make it a practice to try and see every team I broadcast beforehand, even if it's only in practice. At the very least, I'll want to talk with the coach and the publicity director to get a feel for the team. I don't want to go in blind. If you do, it shows. Preparation is the biggest part of the broadcaster's homework. The producer and stage manager can do only so much prompting. Eventually, the show must sink or swim with the announcers, and if they don't know what they're talking about, you know which direction the program is going to take. Straight down.

In the production truck outside the arena, the glamorous world of television isn't so very glamorous. The director and producer sit side-by-side in very tight quarters, with the sound man behind them and other technicians all over the place. There is an air of urgency in there that cannot surface at courtside. There are all kinds of problems. Some are so basic that the ordinary viewer, and even the ordinary broadcaster, would never think of them. The producer, however, must. Something as simple as shooting a pregame graphic—that's a picture that can be flashed on the screen during the opening format—can create headaches if the cameraman is unfamiliar with the players and can't locate the ones the producer wants together.

The director has a bank of five monitors in front of him, each representing a different camera's picture. He selects the one he wants and that choice is shown on a sixth monitor, which is labeled "Program." That's what the audience at home is seeing and that's the picture I have available to me on my courtside monitor. One camera is also used on the scoreboard constantly, and the director can choose to superimpose that scoreboard shot in a corner of the "Program" screen. Usually that's only done in the final minute of each half. That's why I repeat the score as frequently on television as I do on radio. Sometimes the picture the producer or director wants isn't being offered by any of the cameras. Then the truck people will specifically ask for it. Occasionally that will be prompted by something I say. Suppose, for example, I refer to a sign in the stands. The cameramen have no way of knowing I'm talking about that, so the director must request a shot of the sign.

Basketball is a game of numbers, probably more so than any other sport. The listener wants to know what the score is, of course, but he also wants to know how many points the key players have scored, how many fouls they've accumulated, and so forth. That's where the statistician comes in. He must keep a running box score for the play-by-play man, and the system must be simple so that all it takes is a glance to find out the key numbers. With the Knicks I have a regular statistician who works with me every game and knows just what I need and how I like it presented. Each broadcaster has his own idiosyncrasies and "Bullet" Bob Meyer, who works the NBA games at Madison Square Garden, is conditioned to each of them. When Jim Gordon filled in for me on a Knicks broadcast one night, the statistician had to keep the box differently for him.

Each broadcaster must develop his own style. That's something that comes with time. As I said earlier, when I first started I sounded like an echo of three guys—Glickman, Scully, and Keiter. That's not a bad trio to copy, but it wasn't me. I listened to tapes of my broadcasts over and over, trying to develop my own style. Now, I even tape telecasts at home and occasionally I pick up things I never realize I'm doing. One time, for example, I discovered that during the halftime standings show, when I appeared on camera, I was virtually wringing my hands, rotating them over and over. I don't know

Coach George Blaney — Holy Cross (8-) — Left yr.— HC Beat Army in OT at HC 81-77

| Holy Cross | FG's 1 2 3 4 5 | FT's | PF's | total pts |
|---|---|---|---|---|
| 40 Potter — Chris (Co-Capt) 6-8 200 Sr. | 6.7 | 00 00 | 1 3 | 13 |
| 22 Vicens — Michael (Co-Capt) 6-5 185 Sr. | 1 2 3 4 | 88000 00000 00 | 1 2 3 4 | 10 |
| 300'Connor — John 6-8 225 Jr. Woburn, Mass (Woburn HS) | 1 2 3. | 8 0 | 1 2 3 4 | 6 |
| 5 Perry — Ron 6-2 175 Soph. Shrewsbury, Mass. (Catholic Memorial) | 1 2 3 4 5. 6 7 8 | 0 0 0 0 0 0 | 1 2 3 | 10 |
| 14 Beckenbach — Peter 6-3 185 Jr. | | 000 | 1 2 3 | |

For the Coasts three 3rd game in 5 days

Army (8-6) — Coach Mike Krzyzewski (Shu-shev-ski) 3rd year

| Army | FG's 1 2 3 4 5 | FT's | PF's | total pts |
|---|---|---|---|---|
| 52 Brundidge — Clennie 6-4 220 Jr. | 12 | 00 8 | 1 2 3 4 5 | 1 |
| 34 Easton — Scott 6-7 190 Jr. | 1 2 3 4 5 6. | 8. 8 0 | 1 2 3 4 5 | 13 |
| 50 Winton — Gary (Captain) 6-5 220 Sr. | 1 2 3 4 5. 6 7 8 9 10 11 12 13 14 | 0. 8 | 1 2 3 4 5 | 10 29 |
| 30 Brown — Matt 6-5 192 Jr. | 1 2 3 4 5 | | 1 2 3 | |
| 14 Harris — Pat 6-1 173 Jr. | 12 | 000 | 1 2 | 1 |

My quick reference for a Holy Cross-Army game

why it was happening. I'm not a nervous guy, but watching myself do that really aggravated me. I made sure it didn't happen the next week. I sat with my hands folded.

My style of broadcasting basketball depends on enthusiasm and control. I try to capture the excitement of the game with my voice, but at the same time I approach the game with an attitude that nothing that happens on the court can throw me. I've been doing this long enough that I've seen just about everything and feel I can handle whatever will come up. Call it confidence—a broadcaster needs a giant dose of it to be successful. I just feel I have a grip on the situation, much as the all-star guard has a grip on the basketball when he brings it downcourt.

Part of the confidence comes from memorizing a list of phrases I made up for myself when I first started broadcasting. These are my "automatics"—words that come out without me having to think about them. Some of them are words like "rejected," and "stutter-step dribble," or "air ball hits zippo." Another broadcaster I know likes to say "pops" instead of shoots. Someone else might call a basket "bingo"; and my brother Al, when he did games in the old American Basketball Association, which had the three-point basket, had his own. When a player shot one of those longies, he'd call it "downtown," and when a three-pointer went in, it was a "home run."

For me, the phrase I remember best is the one that has become identified with me. I have to admit, I get a kick when college coaches like Digger Phelps at Notre Dame tell me that kids on his team use "Yesss!" all the time in practice. When I hear it and when I use it, I say a private thank-you to my favorite old referee, Sid Borgia.

# PLAY-BY-PLAY
## 2 IN A BROOKLYN BASEMENT

When I was growing up I saw Sid Borgia's act from a variety of spots. There was the balcony at the old Madison Square Garden where I watched the Knicks with my friends, getting into the building on reduced-price tickets which were available through our school. There was the end loge at the Sixty-Ninth Regiment Armory, a dilapidated old National Guard facility, which the Knicks used for a month or so every season when the circus or some other event moved into the Garden. And there was the solitary chair placed just beyond one of the baskets in the Garden, where I sat waiting to corral loose balls when I worked for the team.

For a kid as into sports as I was, I had a ball in my teen-age years. I got to work for the Knicks and also for the old Brooklyn Dodgers, and that gave me an opportunity to rub shoulders with players and front office personnel in both sports. I owe those opportunities to two people—Bones Raleigh, who used to play center for the New York Rangers, and a broadcaster named Howard Cosell, who once did a radio show with kids.

On the streets of Brooklyn (I was born in Manhattan's Beth Israel Hospital in 1943) I played roller hockey as well as basketball, and so I was naturally hung up on the Rangers as much as the Knicks. I often went to practices and interviewed players for my high school newspaper. After all, what could be more fascinating for the student body at Abraham Lincoln High School than reading about the life and times of people like Danny Lewicki and Louie Fontinato?

While I was talking to Raleigh all about the excitement of life in his hometown of Kenora, Ontario, the "regular" writers and broadcasters were dealing with the club's bigger names—people like Coach Alfie Pike. Eventually I noticed one of the radio guys listening in on my conversation with Raleigh. After I finished with Bones, the broadcaster grabbed me. It was Cosell and he asked if I would like to be a panelist on a radio sports show. He did not have to ask twice.

The program was Cosell's first broadcast venture, and it consisted of a group of kids interviewing a sports celebrity. Besides me, the panel included Curt Block, now an NBC executive but at the time ballboy for the Knicks; Joel Schenker, a friend of Curt's who is now president of Kingsborough Community College, and Art Friedman, my boyhood friend who is now the statistician for the Mets and Rangers. Cosell arranged for the guests, and it was a tremendous experience for me because I was so hung up on sports. Nothing was left to chance on the show. Cosell even provided us with the questions. I didn't care, though. I was thrilled at just being in the same studio with all of the big names who appeared on the show.

One time the guest was Fresco Thompson, who was a vice-president of the Dodgers. Now, growing up in Brooklyn, you can understand that the Dodgers were my team. Later I developed an affinity for the St. Louis Cardinals because I was intrigued by one of their journeymen infielders, Solly Hemus. But when Thompson was on the show, the Dodgers were still Number One with me.

After the program was over I somehow got up enough courage to ask Thompson if the club needed any summer help. By some miraculous chance the Dodgers were indeed looking for an office boy. Now that's ridiculous, right? Anyway, Thompson put me in touch with Buzzie Bavasi's secretary (Buzzie was a Dodger executive at the time), and I got the job. I was sitting on Cloud Nine when they hired me. What a great job for a kid.

The Dodger offices were located at 215 Montague Street, and if you saw the place you'd understand why they moved to Los Angeles. They had this old, filthy scoreboard and one of my jobs was to listen to the games on radio—they played mostly day games then—and post the score manually on the scoreboard.

This was 1957—the Dodgers' last year in Brooklyn. The team played 10 or 12 games that year in Roosevelt Stadium in Jersey City and one of my duties was to deliver the tickets on the day of the game to Roosevelt Stadium. All of the tickets. And I didn't go there by cab. I used to take public transportation—the subway, the Hudson Tubes to New Jersey, and then a bus, all the time carrying the tickets for that day's game. I never thought much about it but my father couldn't believe what was going on—that I had all of the tickets, meaning quite a responsibility.

After the games I got to ride back to Brooklyn with the players on the team bus. Sitting next to Gino Cimoli—well, that was just a great thrill for me. I couldn't wait to get home at night to tell my brothers, Al and Steve, about each day with the Dodgers. Often, when the club was playing at home in Ebbets Field, I'd take one of them along to the ball park with me. One of the fringe benefits of my job was two tickets for each home game in the overhanging press box in right field. I went to almost every game and, naturally, I took my tape recorder with me. I did play-by-play broadcasts of virtually every inning the Dodgers played at home that season. Steve or Al would do the color or, if they weren't with me, I'd bring a friend along for that "job."

After the games were over we'd hang around the press box area until Vin Scully, Al Helfer, and Connie Desmond, who were the Dodger announcers in those days, had left for the day. Then we'd go in and gather up scraps of old commercials and statistical handouts to make our next day's "broadcast" that much more realistic.

Now you have to understand that we were not into subtle, toned-down broadcasting. We went at it hot and heavy, screaming into the microphone on each and every play. A routine fly ball might sound something like this:

. . . *Shuba swings . . . and it's a long fly ball . . . deep right center . . . Ashburn racing over . . . and he grabs it on the running track . . . 390 feet from home plate. A good shot by Shotgun Shuba, but just not far enough to get beyond the great speed of Richie Ashburn.*

For Scully, Helfer, or Desmond it probably came out this way:

*. . . Shuba swings . . . fly ball to right center . . . Ashburn moves over and pulls it down.*

You get the idea. We would rant and rave over every play, and we must have been totally obnoxious. I know at least that we certainly were loud. That's because our volume finally got us evicted. Walter O'Malley, owner of the Dodgers then and now, had some friends who used to sit in the same box we did, and when they got tired of listening to our exciting broadcasts, we were told to take our tape recorder elsewhere. Thinking back on it, I can't say that I blame O'Malley's pals for giving us the thumb. I'm sure our presence in their box didn't enhance their enjoyment of the game.

Baseball was a 24-hour-a-day pastime for me in those years. I'd work in the Dodger office in the morning, go to the game in the afternoon, and then spend the evening listening to another game on radio. Or, if there was no game to listen to at night, my brothers and I always had our own league to fall back on. The ABA—Albert Baseball Association—was established with the help of a mail order card game called APBA Baseball. We were what you might call APBA freaks. We were totally hung up on this card game that duplicated the performances of major league players. If Willie Mays had hit 52 home runs the year before for the New York Giants, then you knew if you played the full APBA schedule—and we always did—that Mays was good for 40 or 50 home runs. It was in the cards, and the accuracy of the card performances was so close to the real thing that we were totally and permanently fascinated with the game. We had a full league schedule, and we broadcast all of the games.

I was, of course, a rabid Dodger fan, with one variation. I was also completely taken with Solly Hemus of the Cardinals. Don't ask me why. I really don't know the answer. I just know that he was one of my favorites, and I did for him what any loyal fan would do—I started a fan club. You have to understand that fan clubs were a big hobby for kids in those days. It was no big deal for guys like Duke Snider, Willie Mays, and Mickey Mantle to have them. They were stars. Fan clubs were automatic for them. But Solly Hemus? I had no competition when I decided to start one for my favorite Cardinal infielder. We had a newspaper, the *Hemus Headliner*, and the usual stuff—membership cards, pictures, the whole thing. And when Hemus and the Cardinals visited Ebbets Field, well, it was a grand event for me.

Left: I was born during World War II (1943) and this was taken with my folks (Alida and Max) when my father was serving in the U.S. Army at Fort Bragg, North Carolina.

Right: I took piano lessons at an early age. I'm on the left, Al is in the middle next to baby brother Steve.

Hemus never did very well in our card game baseball league, which probably proves how accurate the game was. But I always gave him a big broadcast buildup every time he came to bat. And when we were at Ebbets Field and the Cardinals were in town, we made sure that Solly knew his fan club was in the stands, rooting for him.

You can imagine that with three sports-crazy boys running around, the Albert household looked like a miniature Madison Square Garden–Ebbets Field all wrapped in one.

My dad, Max, is a native of New York City, so he had something of an understanding about things like the Knicks, Rangers, and Dodgers, the teams that occupied the hearts and minds of his three sons during those growing-up days. Dad occasionally took us to games, but it was difficult to find the time because he owned a retail grocery business with his brother and anybody who does that kind of work can tell you that leisure hours are few and far between.

At first my folks must have wondered what was going on with their boys, who totally inundated the house and their lives with sports. It's certainly not unusual for youngsters to be caught up in sports. But with us it was more than a pastime. It was more like a passion. There were daily schoolyard games at PS 195, sometimes baseball or stickball, sometimes basketball, and sometimes, even a little touch football. And after we played our games, we talked about them. And talked and talked and talked. Mom and dad listened, wondered, shrugged and let us do our thing.

I'd go down to the store sometimes to help stamp cartons or to sit outside and operate my comic book business. I sold regular comics and my own homemade creations to customers as they passed in and out of the store.

Dad recently retired from the grocery business, at the same store he owned when we were growing up. It doesn't take much prodding to get him talking about his sons. Mom watches each of us on television, sometimes when we are head-to-head—with sportscasts on different channels at the same time. And her reaction is typically motherly. "Well," she says, "at least the boys are well."

For every game of baseball, basketball, roller hockey, or stickball that one Albert played, there was another Albert doing the phantom play-by-play broadcasts into the ever-present tape recorder. We even pioneered a play-by-play broadcast that the world of broadcasting still hasn't discovered. Our basement was equipped with a Ping-Pong table, and it was routine for two of the Alberts to be playing a game and the third to be broadcasting it. We may be the only broadcasters in the world prepared and qualified to do table tennis play-by-play when that sport enjoys its move into the big time.

Baseball was fun and roller hockey was great, but when you come right down to it, the Knicks and basketball have always been my Number One passion. I could sit in front of a radio and listen to Marty Glickman and Les Keiter doing play-by-play forever. They simply lifted the listener right out of his seat and made him feel he was sitting right there on the Knicks' bench, next to Coach Joe Lapchick, mapping out last-minute strategy.

Give a kid a basketball and a concrete court and it was magic. Madison Avenue thought it had come up with a marvelous innovation when it introduced one-on-one match-ups between

---

Opposite: One-on-one with Julius Erving. He outscored me, but I blame the referees. (NBC)

NBA stars to spice up halftime shows during televised games. But kids in Brooklyn have been playing one-on-one since Dr. Naismith hung his first peach basket. You be Earl Monroe and I'll be Dr. J. You be Jabbar and I'll be McAdoo or Cowens. It's been going on forever. But when I played it, the guy I wanted to be was Keiter or Glickman. For me, that was where the excitement was.

When the Dodgers and Giants left New York in 1958, Keiter expanded his basketball work into the area of baseball, with broadcast recreations. He would sit in a studio in New York City and receive ticker-tape reports of the play-by-play action. The rest was up to him and his imagination, and he did some job with it. He devised sound effects for the crack of the bat (a pencil against another wooden object), and introduced crowd noise as well with records that supplied cheers when he needed cheers, boos when he wanted boos, and just plain roaring when that was all he required. The effect was devastating, at least on this teen-aged listener.

I decided to visit Keiter in his studio, and he let me watch his operation. It was fascinating, and after he was done, I asked where he had gotten the crowd sounds from. He gave me the name of the company that manufactured the records, and I got the same ones that he was using. After that the Albert Baseball Association broadcasts had sound effects, too.

We had the Hemus fan club to keep us busy in the summer, but the Cardinals never played past September and so basketball got an early start every autumn. Since the Knicks enjoyed a special spot with us, we couldn't wait for the season to start every year. One winter the club came up with a new player who really grabbed me, much the way Solly Hemus had. The new guy was a jump shooter named Jim Baechtold, out of Eastern Kentucky. He had played one season for the Baltimore Bullets before coming to New York, where the headlines belonged to guys like Harry Gallatin, Carl Braun, Sweetwater Clifton, and Ken Sears. Most of them had their own fan clubs. Baechtold had a seat on the bench. He needed a club the same way Solly Hemus had. So Albert, friend of those in need, supplied it.

I hesitate to say this for fear of being accused of patting myself on the back, but of all the Knick-player fan clubs, Baechtold's was the most successful.

The *Baechtold Bulletin* was a basketball version of the *Hemus*

*Headliner*. Anything and everything you could ever care to know about this soft jump shooter from Coraopolis, Pennsylvania, was available. There were monthly meetings, and Baechtold, perhaps a little bewildered by all of the attention he was getting, showed up at many of them, often dragging a teammate along. Bud Palmer, a former Knick player and at that time doing television broadcasts of the team's games, heard about the fan club and plugged us on the air. An artist friend of his designed Baechtold Buttons, which we proudly displayed at every Knick game.

Officials at Madison Square Garden heard about our Baechtold activities and encouraged us. They were grateful for the attention and supplied eight-by-ten photographs and other material. The meetings were the highlight of our month. Mostly they were question-and-answer sessions, and our members always swarmed Baechtold for his autograph. We brought along a camera and started a concession—Take Your Picture With Jim Baechtold. Jim also wrote a column of basketball tips for all the budding Baechtolds. Brooklyn became the jump shot capital of the country, thanks to him.

Eventually the Garden asked me to expand the scope of our fan club and to form one for the entire Knicks team. I jumped at the chance, and it didn't take long for The *Baechtold Bulletin* to be transformed into *Knick Knacks*. We had our fan club meetings on the day of the game, and the Knicks supplied player guests. One of the guards on the club in those days was Richie Guerin, who would later become a basketball color broadcaster. He often reminisces with his play-by-play partner—me—about those old fan club days.

*Knick Knacks* was the culmination of my fan club publications. It was our ultimate newspaper, but it would have been impossible to produce without Aaron Karlin, who operated the School of Popular Music in my neighborhood. I studied piano and accordion at the school and quickly learned that the best mimeograph machine in the neighborhood was owned by Mr. Karlin. He soon became "publisher" of *Knick Knacks*.

At the same time that the fan club was mushrooming, the Garden offered me a spot as a ballboy. In my spot behind the basket I recovered shots and passes that went out of bounds. I was also errand boy, assistant trainer and whatever else they needed me for. It was even better than my office boy job with the Dodgers because now I was really rubbing shoulders—literally, sometimes—with major league athletes. This was the world I had always dreamed about, the world in which I wanted to be. For a kid . . . well, you can understand what all of this meant, being around that scene.

When you're as close to athletes as my jobs with the Dodgers and Knicks allowed me to be, you see everything about them, including the human flaws they share with the rest of us. Some of it was like a study in human nature. I saw how some players dealt with pressure, with success and with failure. I saw some athletes who would stand and sign autographs until every last one of the people who wanted one was accommodated. And I saw athletes brush past fans without signing a single one. All of that gave me a tremendous frame of reference—a feel for the players and for the fans as well. I felt I could relate to both sides—that I could understand the emotions of the players and the demands of the fans. I have used the lessons I learned in those years over and over.

Ballboy Albert is at the end of the bench, next to Ron Sobie. Next to him is Richie Guerin.

After graduating from high school I went to Syracuse University, which has one of the finest communications schools in the East. Among Syracuse's communications alumni is Marty Glickman, and I must admit that I thought about that when I enrolled there. At Syracuse I became involved with live broadcasting for the first time. It was no longer a tape recorder with no one listening. Now it was a microphone with a real audience. It was nervous time for me.

I started out doing rock 'n' roll disc jockeying. You know, the Howl-and-Holler school of broadcasting. . . . "And now . . . Number one on the charts . . . and in your hearts . . . this week . . . " I was the Cousin Brucie Morrow of upstate New York. There was basketball and hockey and some minor league baseball as well. It was a wonderful laboratory in which to smooth out some awfully rough edges in technique, delivery, and all of the elements that go into professional broadcasting.

After my third year at Syracuse, I was offered a job as a writer-producer and back-up announcer at WCBS in New York

And there's Richie Guerin 25 years later as my color man on New York Knicks broadcasts. Statistician "Bullet" Bob Meyer is between us. (RICHARD PILLING)

I owe a lot to Marty Glickman. (WHN)

City. They didn't have to ask twice. I transferred to New York University and started my big city broadcast apprenticeship at the side of one of my real heroes, a consummate professional named Marty Glickman. CBS was doing the Rangers and Knicks in those days with Glickman and Jim Gordon, and I was a program assistant, handing them commercials and trying to help keep the production smooth.

Often I'd take a tape recorder into the press box and do games for myself, the same way I had with the Dodgers in baseball. That's the very best broadcasting experience you can get—doing the job firsthand. I'd listen to my tapes afterward and try to pick out my weak spots—places and ways I could improve my product.

Broadcasting for yourself is one thing. Broadcasting for the public, for an audience that can turn you off at the flip of a switch, is quite another. In January 1963, I went "live" with the Knicks for the first time. Glickman and Gordon were both tied up, and I wound up behind the mike for a game in Boston

Garden. It was the most nervous day of my life when the opening tip-off starting the game was held, and my mike went on for the play-by-play. I somehow survived, though, and I guess the broadcast wasn't a total disaster. Four years later, I was hired to be the voice of the Knicks and Rangers.

Hello there, Mel Allen. He's with Tommy Henrich on Mel Allen Day at Yankee Stadium in 1950. (NEW YORK YANKEES)

# 3 HELLO THERE, EVERYBODY

Growing up in New York City during the 1940s and 1950s was like living in a broadcasting laboratory for someone who had ambitions about making his living behind a microphone. The town was blessed with some of the top professionals in the field during those years, and some skillful dial twirling could deliver an ample supply of all of them.

There could be no better textbook than listening to the work of people like Marty Glickman on basketball and football, Don Dunphy on the Friday night fights, and a host of others who delivered the thrills of their sports into living rooms. Nowhere was the broadcasting talent as concentrated as it was in baseball, because those were the days when three big league teams played in New York.

Yankee fans were treated to the dulcet southern accent of the incomparable Mel Allen, who coined phrases like "a Ballantine Blast" for home runs, and opened his broadcast each day with the familiar "Hello there, everybody." Working alongside Allen in Yankee Stadium were pros like Curt Gowdy, who is now doing cable TV baseball; Jim Woods, now with the Boston Red Sox after stopovers in several other big league towns, and ex-players like Jerry Coleman and the Scooter, Phil Rizzuto.

Over in Brooklyn, we Dodger fans were treated to the old Redhead, Red Barber. A southerner, like Allen, Barber also altered the language of baseball. He coined the word rhubarb to describe those lively discussions that so often punctuated the action at Ebbets Field. If things were going smoothly for the

Red Barber is interviewing Leo Durocher at Ebbets Field on a memorable day, August 26, 1939. This was the occasion of the first televised major league baseball game. The Dodgers played the Reds, and NBC covered it. (NBC)

Dodgers—that was rare—Barber told us that the club "was in the catbird seat" and a home run in those days in Brooklyn was "an Old Goldie," after his cigarette sponsor. Like Allen in the Bronx, Red had some outstanding announcers working with him. Connie Desmond was a longtime partner.

The last addition to the Dodger booth was a young man out of Fordham University. You can measure how good a job Vin Scully did by the fact that he's still broadcasting Dodger games today, two decades later and 3,000 miles away from where he started. And when you go to a game in Dodger Stadium, the ball park echoes with Scully's play-by-play because most of the fans listen to his accounts on transistor radios.

The Giants' broadcaster was the late Russ Hodges, once a partner of Allen's at Yankee Stadium, but for many years the Number One man at the Polo Grounds. His radio account of Bobby Thomson's pennant-winning home run in 1951 is a play-by-play classic. The ironic part is that it would have been lost to posterity had it not been for an industrious Dodger fan who was taping the broadcast and planned to send it to Hodges as one last twist of the knife after Brooklyn clinched the

It all began in Brooklyn for Vince Scully, who went West with the Dodgers. He's flanked by the late Jim Gilliam and Walt Alston. (LOS ANGELES DODGERS)

pennant. When the Giants turned the tables, the fan could have been excused if he set fire to that tape. But he sent it to Hodges anyway, proving his good sportsmanship and making a major contribution to baseball broadcasting history.

When the Giants and Dodgers left New York they took Hodges and Scully with them. Barber moved to the Yankees—a jolt to Brooklyn fans who considered him part of the franchise. Having Barber do Yankee games never seemed to fit, even though he was the man who first dubbed the Stadium. "The House that Ruth Built." Red lasted there until 1965. Then came a collision with management over several issues. Among them, Barber wanted the television cameras to show the empty seats in the ball park, an idea that hardly sat well with the people running the Yankees. Allen was eased out of the broadcast booth that same year. It also marked the start of a 12-year decline of the Yankees, and there are some fans who claim that the team's problems on the field and the dismissal of the two old broadcasting pros in the same year were, in some mystical way, related.

New York's broadcasting alignment for its two baseball teams has been pretty consistent in recent years. Rizzuto is the senior man in the Yankee booth and works with another ex-player, Bill White, and longtime pro Frank Messer. Over at Shea Stadium, the Mets' lineup for 16 years was unchanged with Lindsey Nelson, Bob Murphy, and Hall of Famer Ralph Kiner. Nelson moved to San Francisco in 1979 and was replaced by my brother Steve.

There is an army of ex-players involved in baseball broadcasting. Among them are George Kell and Al Kaline (Detroit), Duke Snider (Montreal), Don Drysdale (California), Jerry Coleman (San Diego), Early Wynn (Toronto), Lou Boudreau (Chicago Cubs), Joe Nuxhall (Cincinnati), Richie Ashburn (Philadelphia), Mike Shannon (St. Louis), Ken Harrelson (Boston), Jim Piersall (Chicago White Sox), Herb Score and Mudcat Grant (Cleveland), Harmon Killebrew (Minnesota), Phil Rizzuto, Bill White, and Fran Healy (New York Yankees), and Maury Wills, Joe Garagiola, and Tony Kubek (NBC).

Some baseball voices, like Barber in Brooklyn and Allen with the Yankees, built a unique identification with their teams. For years, Harry Caray was the voice of the St. Louis Cardinals, and a Pittsburgh game didn't seem official unless Bob Prince was broadcasting it. But times change and Caray and Prince moved on to other cities. It took Cardinal and Pirate fans a while to get over the culture shock of losing those familiar voices.

Caray and Prince have their own unique styles and deliveries, with some "down-home" homilies thrown in that are part of their images. Garagiola is a storyteller. Messer and Nelson are more reportorial in their styles. But there is no right or wrong in baseball broadcasting technique. What's important is that an announcer develops his own image and method and sticks with it. When the late Dizzy Dean did the Game of the Week, it was like talking baseball with some guy pumping gas on a dusty country road. But it worked for Dean and made him successful. There are, however, some basics that any baseball announcer has to follow, whether he's appealing to country folks like Dean, to the big city population like Nelson and Messer, or to the national network audience like Garagiola, Kubek, and Wills.

First of all, you have to consider the nature of the sport. Baseball is a leisurely game, designed deliberately that way to while away a summer's day or night. It is unhurried and the announcer's account of it should fit the nature of the sport—relaxed. The game won't rush by you. There's plenty of time to say everything that needs to be said, so a good rule to follow is to say it. Sometimes I'm envious of baseball broadcasters who have that extra time that hockey, basketball, and even football don't allow.

The best baseball broadcasters I know share a few things that have nothing to do with style or delivery. They do their homework. In that respect, baseball is the same as every other sport. You have to know the teams and players you're talking about. You can have a voice as smooth as Sinatra's, but if you don't know the subject matter, it won't hide inadequacies. So one must come prepared for the game. That means getting to the ball park early to do some legwork around the dressing rooms and dugouts.

A conscientious broadcaster makes it a point to talk to both managers and at least a couple of players before every game. If you're working for one team you'll know what's going on as far as injuries and who's going well or who's slumping. But it never hurts to poke in on the players before the game, just to say hello if nothing else. And when a new team comes to town, you'll want to catch up on how things are going with its players. The dressing rooms and dugouts before the game are the best places for that small talk because the players are loose, free, and easy to talk to for the most part. There's a lot of kibitzing going on, but that's part of the scene. You learn to cut through it and get the information you're after.

We've talked elsewhere about the tools of the trade—the football spotting chart, the rosters and scoring records, and all the rest so important to coverage of other games. But in no sport does the broadcaster use as many tools as he does in baseball. When he arrives in the booth he carries along a library of books and reference materials important to his coverage. Start with the press books published by the individual ball clubs. They contain important records and biographies of each team's players. Add the *Baseball Register*, published each year by *The Sporting News* and containing the lifetime records of every active major leaguer as well as big league managers and coaches. Then you'll want the *Book of Baseball Records*, published by Elias Sports Bureau. This is organized baseball's bible of records, and no game depends more on its statistical history as the one Abner Doubleday—or was it Alexander Cartwright?—invented. *Batting Averages at a Glance* and the *Ready Reckoner*, two more *Sporting News* publications, provide quick reference aids for finding the important numbers while a game is in progress.

*The Sporting News* bills itself as the bible of baseball and it is certainly must reading for any broadcaster working in the sport. So are the daily sports pages and box scores. That's all part of the homework that an announcer must do to stay up to date and, after a while, it becomes automatic. Many announcers will clip newspapers and keep stories catalogued in extensive files. That's a big help when a new team is coming to town and you want to do some catching up on individual players.

In both the press box and the broadcasting booth, writers and announcers covering baseball games all keep their own "scorecards." And there are as many individual systems of scoring a ball game as there are media types covering it. You've probably already developed your own, and it's just as good as mine or anyone else's as long as you can look back at the first inning when the game's in the ninth and still know what happened.

Many broadcasters will list vital statistics like batting averages, home runs, and runs-batted-in next to each hitter's name and won-lost records and earned-run averages next to the pitchers. That's just for convenience and quick reference when you're on the air. The material is available in the daily releases provided before the game by the home club, and it adds a little extra to your account of a game if you can provide up-to-the-minute statistics. Certainly, you should supply them to the listener at least the first time each batter comes to the plate. It gives you one more thing to say during that gap between pitches—the dead time that so many new broadcasters worry about.

Just like scoring systems, there's a good deal of division of duties by broadcast teams around the major leagues. Some clubs have separate crews for radio and television who never switch between the two mediums. Others have a strict rotation setup that moves a broadcaster from radio play-by-play to television color and then to television play-by-play in three-inning chunks. Sometimes the order of rotation is different. It's all up to the individual club's broadcast policies and those of its stations and producers. The order of rotation isn't important. What is important is being able to say the right thing at the right moment, whether on radio or TV.

Baseball radio coverage is much like other sports in that the play-by-play announcer is everything. He must paint the word picture completely, to give his listeners a total view of what is going on. In baseball that even includes the weather, a factor that surfaces in football as well, but is skipped in indoor sports like hockey and basketball. On television, the fans can see if the sun is shining. You don't have to tell them, although it doesn't hurt to point out things like advancing shadows around home plate that could affect the batter's view of the pitch. The same is true of a troublesome sunny field, where a fly ball could be lost in the sun's glare.

Setting the stage on radio usually is the job of one of the broadcasters. On signal from the engineer, he'll open the broadcast with all the background information available, including the starting lineups. He'll talk about the starting pitchers, give the umpire alignment, and other material like that. He'll carry the broadcast through the national anthem and then turn it over to the play-by-play man just before the action begins. To give you the flavor of how a top pro does baseball radio play-by-play, I've borrowed a half inning's worth of Lindsey Nelson's reportage.

*Hello there, everybody. Joaquin Andujar is on the mound for Houston. He is 25 years old, a right-hander from the Dominican Republic. He'll be facing Lee Mazzilli, a switch-hitter batting left. Mazzilli has an eight-game hitting streak going. He's hitting .324, the eighth-leading batter in the National League. He has four homers and 22 runs batted in.*

*Mazzilli has hit safely in 21 of his last 24 games and he has had 19 games this year in which he has had at least two hits. In and waiting . . . here is Andujar with the first pitch of the evening and it is low for a ball. Nick Colosi is calling balls and strikes behind the plate here tonight. In an air-conditioned 72-degree temperature all umpires are working in short-sleeved shirts. And here's the pitch. It's high for a ball. It's 2 and 0. Dal Maxvill is on the coaching lines at third and Denny Sommers is the Met coach at first. Elliott Maddox has moved out on deck for the Mets. Now here's the 2-0. Swung on, hit in the air to center field. Cesar Cedeno is there. And Cedeno makes the catch.*

*One away and Elliott Maddox will be the batter. He is playing third base for the Mets tonight for the second consecutive game. He is hitting .227 and he has eight runs batted in. He's a right-handed batter. Around the infield, Jose Cruz is at first, Art Howe is at second, Roger Metzger is at short and Enos Cabell is at third. The pitch is in for a called strike. Dennis Walling is in left field. Cesar Cedeno is in center and Terry Puhl is in right. Andujar's pitch is . . . outside and low for a ball. It's 1-1. Bruce Boisclair is out there on deck. It has been a warm, humid day in Houston. Here's the 1-1 . . . outside and low for a ball. It's bat night here in the Astrodome. Here's a swing and a foul ball off and out of play. It's two balls and two strikes. Fans coming into the park receive a coupon and the coupon can be exchanged for a bat as they leave the stadium, after the game. Saves wear and tear on the seats, and that sort of thing. Two balls and two strikes to Elliott Maddox. The pitch is high and off the glove of Ferguson. The count is full at three and two. The outfield defense is straightaway. Andujar is poised for the payoff pitch and it's on the way . . . swung on . . . hit on the ground toward third . . . cut off by Andujar . . . he bobbles it . . . has no play and Elliott Maddox is on at first. Andujar came up and is charged with an error. He made a stab at the ball—two-handed stab—and when it squirted away from him, he simply stood frozen with his arms at his side in some disgust and no play was made on Maddox as he crossed the bag at first.*

*That brings up Bruce Boisclair hitting .203 for the year, one homer and six runs batted in. He bats left. At first base, Jose Cruz is holding against the runner. Bob Watson out of the lineup with a thumb that has troubled him for a couple of years. There's a pitch in for a called strike, 0-1. Steve Henderson is out there on deck. Boisclair takes a look down to the third base coach, Dal Maxvill. Now Maddox takes his lead. And the pitch is low for a ball, 1-1. The Mets are batting here in the top of the first inning. Andujar looks to Ferguson, now sets and checks back over his shoulder. Swing and a ground ball to second. Taken there by Howe, over to short to Metzger and the throw back to first . . . double play . . . second to short to first, Howe to Metzger to Cruz, and the side is retired. There were no runs, no hits. There was an error. None were left and in the middle of the first inning, the score is the Mets nothing and the Astros coming to bat.*

Now that's the consummate professional at work. The delivery is smooth, comfortable, uninterrupted, even though, by its very nature, there are obvious gaps in the action. The question that has always troubled every play-by-play announcer who ever slid in behind a microphone is "What do I say between pitches?" But it's not only a question of what you say. It's how you say it. It's the ability to make the sequence smooth so the listener is unaware of the breaks.

Lindsey Nelson likes to tell the story about a young man who went to Fordham University—Vin Scully's alma mater—and spent quite a bit of time around Shea Stadium. He wanted to be a baseball announcer and one day he came up to Lindsey and told him that Jim Thompson, a Met vice-president, had given him permission to take a tape recorder into the broadcast booth and do a game. "Well, sir," remembers Nelson, "afterward he had the most perplexed look on his face and he asked me, 'What do you do between pitches?' Well, sir, that's the whole trick. That's the job. It's very seldom that anyone has any problem with the actual description of the action.

"Football doesn't pose that problem. You know that they are going to snap the ball every 30 seconds. But in baseball, you get a tough situation and that guy on the mound is going to walk around and take his time. That's when it gets tough.

"Another problem is the rain delay. On radio, you normally throw it back to the station, but on television you stay at the park on the theory that you will never get your audience back if you release them. AstroTurf has complicated this problem because it only takes a few minutes to sweep the rain off. In Cincinnati, for example, they rarely lose a game to rain and they wait until three in the morning if they have to. It would help to know how long you were going to have to fill. There are times when you've said just about everything that you can say but you have to stay with it—and find something else to say.''

So the trick is to pack as much information and anecdotes as you can into your head to have it available when you need something. Sometimes you store material for years before you use it. For example, on the Mets' first trip to Atlanta during the 1978 season, Jerry Koosman started one of the games for New York. During the game Nelson told a story about how Koosman had once spent an off-season in Atlanta, working for the Georgia Power and Light Company. Lindsey got quite a bit of reaction to the story. What the listeners didn't know was that he had learned about the pitcher's unusual winter job nine years before during a casual conversation over breakfast. He just stored the story away to be used at an appropriate time.

That's the advantage of being a team announcer working with the same club and the same players day-in and day-out. Doing a club, an announcer becomes involved firsthand. He is identified with that team. People asked Lindsey Nelson if he was a Met fan, and he told them he certainly was. He wanted them to win and I can't blame him for that. You try not to have that come across on the air but there isn't a team announcer I know who wouldn't prefer to see his team win instead of lose. That's just human nature.

Some announcers aren't comfortable with the single team identification of an Ernie Harwell with the Tigers or a Scully with the Dodgers. For those guys, the network game-of-the-week assignments are ideal. But announcers don't always have their choice. My play-by-play baseball debut came in a somewhat more intimate setting, though. After my freshman year at Syracuse University I got a summer job broadcasting the games of the old Syracuse Chiefs of the International League, on WFBL. In those days the Chiefs were operated jointly by the Minnesota Twins and Washington Senators, and our roster showed it. There is no chance that any of those Chiefs will ever be immortalized in baseball's Hall of Fame, but for a young man just getting his feet wet in broadcasting, their names will never be forgotten.

The first baseman was Frank Leja, who failed his share of trials with the New York Yankees. The second baseman was Ted Lepcio, a dropout from the Philadelphia Phillies. At shortstop we had journeyman Willie Miranda and the third baseman was a career minor leaguer named Woody Smith. Joe Altobelli, who later became manager of the San Francisco Giants, was our left fielder, with Dan Dobbek, who had a couple of cups of major league coffee in center, and the marvelously named Angel Scull in right. Dutch Dotterer, a magic name in that era, was our catcher. The pitching staff included former and future big leaguers like Lee Stange, Gerry Arrigo, and Bob Porterfield. The manager was Frank Verdi, and he was the target of a brief and abortive player revolt led by Porterfield, who felt he was better suited to fill out the lineup card. Instead, Porterfield was invited to seek employment elsewhere.

Syracuse had two good prospects who the manager wasn't allowed to play. The front office was afraid that other clubs would get wind of Jimmie Hall and Rich Rollins and draft them, so they sat to keep them hidden. But it didn't work, and they went on to become solid major leaguers.

The International League in those days had some pretty good ballplayers. Boog Powell was a Baltimore prospect at Rochester and was one of the IL's top runs-batted-in men. Another was Luke Easter, a major league hero of another era. Tom Tresh was at Richmond, being prepped for the Yankees. The big news for us that summer was the acquisition of Lepcio, who carried instant credibility because of his status as an ex-major leaguer.

Now you must understand that for the people of Syracuse, the Chiefs were big league. And for me to be broadcasting their games—well, let me tell you, I popped a few buttons when I got that job. We broadcast all the home games live, and we also carried all of the road games, re-creating the play-by-play by use of the Western Union ticker service. Like Easter and some of those IL stars, re-creation broadcasts are of a bygone time in radio baseball. It's a shame, really, because they tested the ingenuity of the broadcaster to capture the excitement of a game that he cannot see. You've got to embellish on bare bones of information, which was all the ticker provided. It was a terrific method to improve broadcasting technique.

Anyway, we were in the summer of 1961 when the big news in baseball was the home-run battle being waged by New York Yankee teammates Roger Maris and Mickey Mantle. Both were challenging the single-season record of 60 homers set by another Yankee slugger, Babe Ruth. For a while it seemed both Maris and Mantle would shatter the barrier and, as you can well imagine, the baseball world was wrapped up in the struggle of the two modern sluggers to break one of the game's most revered marks. It was, to say the very least, a big story.

The fans in upstate New York were able to follow the Mantle–Maris duel on a small FM station that was hooking into the Yankee broadcast network. But the major station in town was "WFBL, home of the International League Chiefs where you can follow the play-by-play action of every game, home and away, with Peter Scott and Marv Albert."

Peter Scott was the radio name of my partner, Carl Eilenberg, on those broadcasts; he now owns a radio station in upstate New York. Carl and I shared one of broadcasting's most embarrassing moments—embarrassing and humbling.

The Chiefs were on the road one day in September and we were in the studio doing our re-creation broadcast. We were surrounded with the paraphernalia required for those shows— the fan noise records for background sounds, the two pencils used to simulate the crack of the bat, the score sheets, record books, and the like. Eilenberg was doing the play-by-play when he made one of those blunders that baseball broadcasters have nightmares about. He lost two innings.

The game was sailing along in the third inning when, suddenly, he had it in the fifth. There was no way to solve the dilemma. We had blown two innings of play-by-play detail. We just plowed ahead, waiting for the station switchboard to light up with listeners asking how Angel Scull had done in the fourth inning. The only thing worse than the two missing innings would be the reaction of our listeners. There was none.

Not one phone call came in to protest the absence of those two innings of action. What had happened was that the fans had become more caught up in the Mantle–Maris home-run derby than they were in the fortunes of the hometown Chiefs, and they had twirled their dials over to the FM station to listen to the Yankees. We were on the biggest station in town but our audience was missing in action. It gave the hometown broadcasters pause for thought.

Baseball was the first sport I ever broadcast professionally, so it will always occupy a warm spot with me. Remember, that while growing up, it was the first sport I practiced broadcasting, and I had plenty of experience at it when I auditioned for the Syracuse job. I remember the tape I submitted to get the job was one of an old Brooklyn-Pittsburgh game. When I was hired, I was on a cloud and when one of our guys made it to the majors, well, that made me proud. I felt I had a little part of that player, and I guess that's how it is when you're doing every game for a club.

I think baseball is the toughest sport to be really good at. If you're doing a club that isn't a contender, it's a long season, a very long season. That's why I admire the pros in our business who are able to handle that burden and still hold the interest of the fans.

On the set at NewsCenter4 with Chuck Scarborough and Jack Cafferty. (RICHARD PILLING)

# 4 THE DAILY SHOW

The easiest part of my day is the three or four minutes that I spend on camera, reporting the sports news each afternoon and evening. It's less than 300 seconds of air time, and it represents the culmination of a lot of difficult work by many talented people, craftsmen at their trade, who are vital to the success of the sports spot. There are cameramen, technicians, film and tape editors and so many others who play a role in the creation of those few minutes of air time. The difficult work comes before, putting the show together, assigning crews, making sure all the important sports news is covered. Once it has been packaged, the easy part is putting it to the public on the air.

Most television stations have adopted the easy, informal setting that creates a pleasant situation for both the viewer and the sportscaster. The introduction to sports is handled by the anchorman who, not so long ago, had to deliver the sports news along with the weather forecast and the rest of the show's package. Now there are specialists to handle the nonhard news segments and that's the way it should be. You wouldn't expect a newspaper's lead columnist to be writing the lead sports story, so why should the TV anchorman be delivering scores and the rest of the "back page" news?

The format on NBC's NewsCenter4 has anchorman Chuck Scarborough or Jack Cafferty introducing me with the camera peeking over my shoulder at them. That is the director's way of placing me on the set. It is a comfortable approach that eases my introduction on the screen and avoids jarring the audience with a sudden switch from the anchorman to me.

A successful sports broadcaster can't be what people in our business call "a rip and read guy." That refers to an announcer who is content to tear off wire service stories by the Associated Press and United Press International and read that raw copy on the air. First of all, AP and UPI correspondents are writing their stories for the eye. A sports broadcaster's means of communication is the ear. So the least he can do is rewrite the wire dispatches, tailoring them for audio use. Sometimes, though, in the last-second rush before a show goes on the air, a late-breaking story comes in and there is just no time to do anything with it. Your first responsibility, always, is to get the news to your listeners and if sometimes you have to "rip and read" to accomplish that, then you rip and read. The important thing is to avoid making a habit of depending on the wire services for your stories. You have to get out of the office on the sports beat.

When a newspaper reporter is sent on assignment, all he needs is his pen, a notebook, and his typewriter. But a broadcaster on assignment comes complete with a two- or three-man camera crew lugging lights, battery packs, tripods, and all sorts of equipment. Covering a story for the print media is considerably less complex, at least in terms of the accompanying paraphernalia that must be brought along. What's more, the print journalist approaches the story from a different perspective. The television sportscaster must always be thinking visually. I'll give you an example.

When Roy Boe decided to move his National Basketball Association franchise from Long Island to New Jersey, the news conference announcing the switch was held at Giants Stadium in the Meadowlands sports complex. That site was selected because Boe's decision to move the Nets was based in part on a committment from the New Jersey State Sports Authority to construct a 20,000-seat basketball facility at the Meadowlands. For the print journalists, the story that day was centered on the comments of Boe, Sonny Werblin, then chairman of the Sports Authority, and Brendan Byrne, governor of the state. But for television, one-on-one interviews with three executives could become pretty boring. So I dispatched my camera crew to the outside of Giants Stadium for some shots of the exterior. That gave the flavor of what the Authority had done to lure a football team across the Hudson and showed one of the selling points Werblin had used in convincing Boe to follow.

When I got back to the studio to edit my tape, I spiced it up with some footage of Julius Erving playing for the Nets. Dr. J. was gone from the team, but he remained its image, and the memory of what had been during his glory years with the team provided a poignant commentary to the simple, straightforward report of Boe's decision to move.

The finished product seen on the 6 or 11 o'clock news takes some time to assemble. There is editing and patching of various segments, with cues that have to fit perfectly, like the pieces of a complex jigsaw puzzle. One of the pieces is the interview, perhaps the most important element of the show. Viewers want to know the scores and the news, it's true. But they are also interested in the personalities who make that news. That's where the interview comes in.

Sportscasters have two ways to get interview features. They can either schedule a film crew to go out to a news conference or a sports event and do it on the subject's location, or you can arrange for the subject to come to the studio. At NewsCenter 4, studio time is available every day for taping interviews, and it's a lot easier to work under those conditions than it is to try and create the technical arrangements necessary for a professional

In the control room, the director—he's in the middle—has a couple of dozen television monitors to choose from. He's the one who decides, among other things, which camera shot you're going to see on your screen. (RICHARD PILLING)

job in the field. In the studio we have all of the technical refinements we need to do a proper job. On location, you do the best you can with portable equipment.

On assignments outside the studio, the station generally sends a three-man crew with the broadcaster, who is called "the talent." One man will handle the camera, another the audio, and a third the lights. It takes a while for the crew to get set up, and I'll usually spend that time with the subject of the interview, chatting. That serves two purposes. It puts the subject at ease and gets him prepared for the questions I'll be asking him when the film begins to roll.

Interviewers use different techniques for asking their questions. Some will use a script with questions scribbled on it. A few rely on the flow of the conversation, which can be dangerous if your subject turns out to be a dud. I know one broadcaster who used a blackboard in the studio and positioned it behind the subject. In that way, when he looked at the guy he was interviewing, he had a homemade prompter right in his line of vision. That's a bad idea as far as I'm concerned.

The studio setting, like NewsCenter4's "Five Minutes" segment, generally is a simple one-on-one arrangement with broadcaster and subject seated in a relaxed manner, just chatting. The interview in the field gets away from that living-room arrangement, and we try to show where we are. We might as well, as long as our crew is leaving the studio.

In the studio, things like voice levels for the audio track are taken care of in the control room with no interruption. Outside, the sound man must constantly check for it and be concerned with other noises that mix into the sound track. Visually, there are differences, too. In the studio, there are few camera complications. Outside, the cameraman must scramble for position, and sometimes that's no easy chore. It wasn't an interview situation, but let's not forget how Woody Hayes swung at an ABC cameraman at the 1977 Ohio State–Michigan game. It should cost coaches who pull that stuff at least 15 yards.

One of the techniques used in film or tape interviews is to show the broadcaster by himself, speaking to the subject who is off camera. Well, here's a secret. Those are manufactured shots. With a single cameraman, he can't be taking shots from different positions. So what we do is film the interview straightaway from top to bottom. Then, when that's finished and

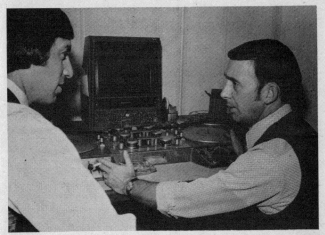

This is the room where the film editing is done. (RICHARD. PILLING)

the subject is off talking to other newsmen or broadcasters, we'll shoot cutaways to edit into the piece. I'll repeat one or two of the questions while the cameraman shoots me full face. It seems like I'm talking right at the subject, but he's really long gone. Sometimes those cutaways involve shots of the broadcaster listening to replies with the voice of the subject played over it.

These are techniques borrowed from the motion picture industry. They do the very same things in the movies, and I think people in the television business are more aware of these kind of things than the general public. If it's done right it can be a very effective and useful change of pace for your interview. But too often it looks staged.

There are two technologies we can deal with for the out-of-the-studio interview. One is tape and the other is film. And, as in most areas where you have a choice, there are advantages and disadvantages for both techniques. Tape is instant and film is not. When I use tape, the cassette is usually waiting for me to edit when I get back to the office. Film must be developed and that takes time. But tape editing at this point is much more difficult. You can still do more complex things with film than you can with tape. Tape quality usually looks better and is being refined all the time.

The use of tape cassettes is called electronic journalism, and it is a major part of our business. Without it you'd be watching a broadcaster reciting scores for those 300 seconds, and it wouldn't take long for you to tire of that. With electronic journalism, the options of a broadcaster are expanded tremendously.

Film and tape are to a television broadcaster what photographs are to a newspaperman. They dress up a presentation, make it more interesting and appealing to the eye. And, after all, the eye is what television is all about. The medium caters to the sense of sight. That's why the video side of the sports show is so important.

I can write a two- or three-minute sports show script in perhaps a half hour. But it takes much longer than that to arrange the video portions of my report. I'll sit with a stopwatch in a screening room and watch a piece of tape maybe 10 or 15 times, editing it for my show. I might want only 20 or 30 seconds' worth of tape to illustrate a particular segment, but choosing *which* 20 or 30 seconds is the hard part.

We have a library of films and tape called "Sports Hold" footage which is available to us. This is video material of past events that is kept in sort of a library from which something can be drawn at any time. When Dave Kingman made his first appearance at Shea Stadium after being traded by the Mets, we went to the Sports Hold footage for tape of Kingman hitting a home run. When Rod Gilbert was shoved into retirement by the New York Rangers, my audio report was backed by tape of a Gilbert goal. You can see how effective that kind of visual approach can be to a sports show.

Let's take the Kingman tape as an example of how we edit tape. I decided that I wanted 20 seconds' worth of tape of one of his homers. I consulted our master index list of Sports Hold footage for a Kingman home run. Each piece of tape or film in our library has an identifying number and a line or two of description so that the broadcaster can quickly locate the material he wants. I call down to the library and they send the appropriate Kingman tape to the screening room. There, two technicians will cue up the tape so that it can be rolled as soon as I get there.

Now, if I want 20 seconds of Kingman, I'll edit 22 seconds. The extra couple of seconds is called a "tail," and it gives you an overlap, sort of a margin for error. Cutting the tape to precisely

20 seconds would be too chancy. This way, if the video switch from tape to studio is a second or two slow, no great damage is done.

I'll sit with a stopwatch and view the tape, deciding which 20 seconds I want. I might decide to take Kingman's swing, the view of the ball dropping over the fence and then his home-run trot, cutting him as he rounds second base. Or I could start with his swing, then the outfielder at the fence, watching the home run, and finally Kingman trotting home. The second, obviously, is a bit more complex since it involves eliminating the portion of the tape that follows him around the bases. What is used is entirely up to the individual broadcaster, who may in some cases consult with a producer on the selection. Sports producer Bill Brown or Len Zaslowsky edits most of my game highlights. I prefer to edit the interview and feature portions.

As the tape rolls, the parts I want are dubbed from the Sports Hold reel onto a second reel. This second reel is the one that will be used when we are on the air, and it will be rolled from the same screening room where I view it and edit it. The editing room is the nerve center of a broadcast's video portion. It is in this room that the show succeeds or fails, and much of that success or failure depends on the skill of the technicians you work with and your feel for editing the material.

I first like to watch an entire piece of tape from start to finish, timing particular segments. For example, on the Kingman tape, I'll break the tape down, seeing how much time each sequence takes. That helps me decide how much I can include. The first time through, you think in terms of starting and stopping points. You don't want to jar the viewer. I like to make as smooth a transition as possible from the tape segment back to the studio.

While you're editing you must also remember to think in terms of "In Cues" and "Out Cues"—the audio signals that will tell the director and technicians when to roll the video sequence. And you must remember to arrange for "Supers," which are superimposed words identifying the tape. In the case of the Kingman tape, the Supers would read Dave Kingman, and, Courtesy of WOR-TV, identifying the subject and crediting the Mets' local TV station, which shot the tape originally and made it available to us.

Film is much easier to edit than tape. The strip you're working from is simply run through a movie editor, a hand-cranked machine that is almost identical to the ones that camera hobbyists use at home. There is a numbering sequence which corresponds to the frames of film, and the editing is done by simply starting at a particular frame and number and stopping on a voice or time cue which is prearranged between the broadcaster and technicians.

Tape is considered to be the wave of television's future and will eventually be the source of all electronic journalism because it is faster and cheaper to work with than film. Improvements are being made in the technical aspects of tape all the time and eventually the only film we'll use is on old events where tape simply isn't available. For me, though, there is something romantic about watching the fuzzy film image of old football or baseball games. There is a certain flavor to that product that clear, crisp tape can't capture.

After I'm through preparing the tape and film for my show, it's time to write the script. A TV script is divided in half on the page, one side for video cues and the other for the actual verbal portion. I figure that each page of script equals about 20 seconds of air time, and I work within those limits.

Writing the script is easy. I start with the day's hard news, the results if games have been played, news of a trade or signing or whatever qualifies as the top sports story of the day. From there I work into the news of the New York local teams . . . if the Yankees and Mets are playing that night during the summer, or the Knicks, Rangers, Islanders, or Nets are scheduled during the winter. Mondays usually have lighter programming than the rest of the week and that gives me a good chance to catch up on the busy weekend action, especially during the pro football season, when there always seems to be some lively NFL material produced.

When the script is completed, it is submitted to the production office. I keep one copy to work from on the set. Two copies go to the director and the assistant director, and a fourth is transcribed on to the teleprompter. Many broadcasters depend on the teleprompter, which provides a slowly advancing script, handwritten in large block letters and moving at a comfortable pace, to be read on the air. I do not use one simply because I prefer to look up and down at my script. I don't feel it interferes with my delivery and, in fact, I think it might even help in some ways. I'd be uncomfortable looking at the camera all of the time.

Before I go on camera I have to visit the makeup room, where

That's what a teleprompter looks like. I'm more comfortable without it. (RICHARD PILLING)

a cosmetician applies coloring to my face so that it will blend with the harsh lights that television requires. The cosmetician works in a small room a few hundred feet down the hall from the news studio, and if it wasn't for the setting, you'd think you were walking into a posh barber shop or beauty salon. The makeup person works with makeup and hair spray, and when they're finished you're ready to face the camera's eye.

Perhaps five or seven minutes before my segment goes on the air, I'll arrive at the control room. There a small microphone that looks like a tie clasp is attached to my necktie and my ear-plug hookup with the director is arranged. That's to provide instant communication in case of a late-breaking story or for any stage directions it may be necessary to relay to me.

Finally, the anchorman says the usual, "Back in a moment, after these messages," and it's time to move onto the set. While commercials are occupying the air time, I'll slip behind a desk across the set from the anchorman. We'll chat for a moment or two about nothing terribly important, and in no time the voice from the control booth comes on. "Ten seconds to air, guys." The next thing you know, the red light on the camera is on and the anchorman is saying those familiar words.

"And now, here with the sports is Marv Albert."

Veteran Marty Glickman works a football game. Thanks to him, I got my first football assignment as a professional.

# 5 THE WHOLE WORLD ISN'T WATCHING

*A* sportscaster needs more than just a microphone to do his job. There are other tools in this trade that are every bit as vital as the electronic ones in the creation of a good presentation. Press guides and player registers that supply facts and figures about the athletes with career records and other pertinent material are important aids a broadcaster refers to frequently. I'm never without an *NHL Guide* at a hockey game or NBA record book for a pro basketball game. And in football, which is, perhaps, the most complex sport of all to broadcast, we use the same kinds of reference books.

When Walter Payton is ripping up huge chunks of yardage or Bert Jones is completing a string of passes, the broadcaster has to be able to point out what the record is and how close Payton or Jones is to it. And, when Lyle Alzado or Harvey Martin is breaking up play after play and recording a fistful of sacks, the play-by-play man has to be aware of how many tackles they have and how they are controlling the flow of play. That's where his helpers come in—the reference guides and record books and the statisticians and spotters who work in the booth with the broadcaster.

When you hear a broadcast at home you're only aware of the play-by-play announcer and the color man. The others are silent partners, but the spotters and statistician are vital to the success of a show. All those little numbers that a broadcaster casually tosses your way are courtesy of his statistician—such as my boyhood friend, Art Friedman, who does that job for the New York Rangers and New York Mets, and "Bullet" Bob Meyer, the Yonkers Raceway track announcer who often works with me in the booth at New York Knicks and Ranger games. And on football broadcasts, those stat men are joined by spotters who help separate the bodies in those pileups, sometimes before the officials can.

Football spotters work with a spotting chart which they share with the play-by-play broadcaster. In the broadcast booth the spotter for one team will sit on the play-by-play man's right and the spotter for the other team will sit at his left. In front of them are the charts that list the formations of their team. On one side is the offensive alignment and on the other side is the defensive setup. These are sometimes called flip cards, and writers also use them although they are smaller and more compact than the ones the broadcast media work with.

Made up well before game day, our spotting charts are written on with dark, easy-to-read, felt marking pens. Each player is listed at his position along with his height, weight, school, and NFL experience. In smaller, lighter print, we include the name of his backup. Sometimes we add important extra facts. Under Martin's name, for example, it might say, "Led NFL with 23 sacks last season." Under Payton's, it would say, "The 1977 NFL rushing champion." When a play is run, it is the spotter's responsibility to point to the men involved on his chart. The play-by-play man may not always look for or need the help—we do see a few plays ourselves, you know—but it's good to know that an experienced spotter is seated alongside you, ready to supply names.

Spotting is especially tough on defense when there are so many pileups. Sometimes the defensive spotter will point to two or three players on his chart to indicate the first men in on the stop. On offense, the spotter will often point to a lineman who threw a key block, opening up a hole for the ball-carrier. Information like that adds a necessary touch to the broadcast.

Football broadcasting is similar to basketball in that there is a world of difference between doing the sport on radio and doing it on television. On radio you are saying everything—setting formations, reporting the progress of the play, whether it succeeds or fails, how much it gains or loses, and getting the color man in for his commentary as well. It's nonstop narrative. But on television, what you say is minimal compared to radio play-by-play. Just like basketball on TV, you leave out the obvious that would be an important part of radio play-by-play. On television, for example, you would never use the phrase,

WR
Paul Warfield 42 (Though has half injury) (self-pacer slick quick) 6' 18? Ohio St. (13)
Dave Logan 85 (wicked middle linebacker) 6'4, 224, Colorado (2)

LT
Doug Dieken 73 (speed inside 1956 pass) 6'3, 252, Illinois (6)
Bob Lingenfelter 75 6'7, 277 Nebraska (e)

LG
Henry Sheppard 65 6'4, 296 SMU (2)
Al Dennis 62 6'4, 250 Grambling (3)

C
Tom DeLeone 54 (Danielson) 6'3, 249 Ohio St (6)
Gerry Sullivan 79 6'4, 250 Illinois (4)

RG
Robert Jackson 68 6'3, 260 Duke's
Al Dennis 62 6'4, 250 Grambling (3)

RT
Barry Darrow 63 6'7, 260 Montana (3)
Bob Lingenfelter 75 6'7, 277 Nebraska (2)

TE
Gary Parris 84 6'2, 226 Florida St (5)
Oscar Roan 81 6'4, 214 SMU (3)

QB
Dave Mays 10 6'1, 204 Texas Southern
Terry Luck 7 (signed as FA last year) 6'3, 205 Nebraska (1)
Brian Sipe 17 6'1, 195 San Diego St (4)

RB
Greg Pruitt 34 5'10, 190 Oklahoma
Larry Poole 38 6'1/2, 185 Kent St

RB
Cleo Miller 30 5'11, 202 Arkansas AM
Mike Pruitt 43 (No. 1 last yr) 6' 214 Purdue (2)
Brian Duncan 35 6' 201 SMU (2)

WR
Reggie Rucker 33 6'2 190 Boston U. (6)
Ricky Feacher 83 5'10, 174 Mississippi

Here is a typical chart that I prepared—covering the Cleveland Browns' offense

"Signals being called," but on radio that is a vital piece of your report to indicate the progress of the action and that the play is about to be run. On TV you don't have to tell the viewer that. He can see it for himself.

Here are examples of the differences in reporting the same play, first on radio and then on TV:

*First and 10 at the Raiders' 30 . . . Stabler brings his team to the line of scrimmage . . . The set backs are Clarence Davis and Mark van Eeghen . . . Cliff Branch and Fred Biletnikoff flanked left and right . . . Stabler ducks in over his center . . . Calling signals . . . Back to throw . . . Pitches instead to Davis . . . Finds a hole behind Upshaw's block for three, four, five yards . . . Pulled down by Greene . . . It will be second and five from the Oakland 35.*

On TV the commentary would be much briefer. The picture tells the story.

*Oakland goes to work at its own 30, first down . . . Stabler at quarterback with Davis and van Eeghen behind him . . . Branch flanked left and Biletnikoff right . . . Stabler looking . . . Davis . . . Goes for five . . . Greene on the tackle . . . A good block by Upshaw opened the hole for Davis . . . It will be second and five from the Oakland 35.*

Football is a television game. Isolating individual players provides an insight for viewers. The instant replay gives the audience a second and often a third look at the play in slow motion, reducing the action to a speed that can be handled by the eye. It breaks down the action. You can see an offensive lineman holding. You can see a guard blowing out the defensive line to open the hole. You can see pass interference in the secondary. And in every case, you can see it much more clearly through the camera's eye than you can with the human eye.

Because you have the camera doing so much of your work, the television play-by-play broadcaster's role is reduced compared with the workload he must carry on radio. On television the play-by-play and color man can just about share the air with a 50-50 split. The camera gives you more time to talk. But on radio, the play-by-play man must dominate. He supplies the excitement that the camera provides and captures so well on television.

Of course, because the medium offers so much more in its coverage, more work goes into the planning of the production. Nothing you see on a televised football game is impromptu. Everything is preplanned. The day before the game a production meeting is held, during which feature items are discussed and thoughts exchanged among all hands involved in the broadcast. Everybody contributes, and the result is an improved production.

Suppose, for example, the color commentator on a particular game is Len Dawson. Besides his career as a first-rate quarterback, Lenny was placekicker Jan Stenerud's holder. When Dawson retired, Stenerud's kicking suffered. The two clearly were linked. Dawson attacked the holding job as a science. He knows what kickers and holders are thinking about. Somewhere in the game we'll isolate on a snap and that will be one of our quick, 20-second features. It's an opportunity for Dawson to display his expertise and adds another dimension to the coverage.

Television production men like to do things like that. It dresses up the show, but putting material like this together is no simple matter. It all starts at that meeting where the TV team designs its own game plan for the coverage. It's a brain-picking session with all hands contributing. And there are plenty of hands. Television football is like a Hollywood spectacular. It seems like there's a cast of thousands involved, even though the viewer may only be aware of the two or three booth broadcasters.

Little things add so much to the presentation. There are graphics, for example. Dozens of simple facts are set up in advance to be shown at the appropriate time. Suppose a receiver like Harold Carmichael is working on a long string of catches. We'll set up a graphic that reads: "Carmichael has caught at least one pass in 78 straight games." When Carmichael makes his catch, we're ready with that graphic. Suppose New Orleans has had scoring problems in the third quarter. We'll set one up that says: "That was New Orleans' second TD in the third quarter this season." When it happens, if it happens, our graphic goes on the screen. Then there are any number of statistical combinations that are always available.

Things like "Six carries, 21 yards," which can be superimposed under a running back in his three-point stance.

There are some basic things that we do on a broadcast. Lineups, for example. I try to mention the names of the players on the field at least once or twice a quarter. If you don't, there is a tendency to overlook important aspects of the game, such as the play of the offensive line. On radio, the lineups are even more important because the broadcaster is the eyes of his listener. If you don't mention who's playing, how will he know? Because of the total verbal medium, the lineups have an extra meaning on radio, and so I try to report them more frequently. I'll also supply the time remaining on radio more often, a job the TV graphics take care of with the superimposing of the stadium clock at the corner of the screen.

In radio, you work harder, but technically it's much simpler than television. There's less that can go wrong when you're dealing with audio alone instead of with visual technique and audio as well. After a radio broadcast, I'm exhausted. Television, for the broadcaster, is easier. For the technical crew, however, it's a lot tougher.

One of the advantages of television broadcasting is stadium location. It is a fact of life that TV gets a better broadcast spot than radio. In plenty of ball parks where I've worked, radio locations are really bad. I've done a lot of games standing up, simply because I couldn't see the action that well sitting down. Shea Stadium has an awful radio broadcast location for football, while the new Giants Stadium in New Jersey may be the best broadcast facility for both radio and TV in the entire league.

At halftime on television, the broadcast switches back to the studio for scoreboard shows such as "The NFL '79" on NBC, and that's time for a breather for the guys in the booth. At halftime on radio you sometimes switch back to the studio for news, but you are often locked into interviews that keep you going during that intermission period. There's no time to recoup and talk things over the way you can in TV.

Football is a unique game to cover. It requires more preparation than any other sport because you're dealing with two teams of 45 players each—offensive, defensive, and special teams—and the technical strategies employed in different situations. If you don't do your homework before doing a broadcast, it is immediately evident. That's the minus. The plus is that you have plenty of time to prepare because teams play only one game a week. And that's what makes each weekend's action so exciting. Each game is magnified in importance when you're only playing 16 in a season instead of 162, the way they do in baseball.

So how do you do your homework? Well, there are a variety of ways. Make it a point to talk to the public relations people of both teams. Find out what has been going on with their teams. You want to know more than won–lost records and point totals, for that's available from newspaper agate. You want to know about lineups, position changes, who's playing well and who's not—the kind of information that builds an interesting broadcast. Most broadcasters also receive the sea of news releases and statistical rundowns produced each week by both the National Football League and its individual clubs. These are often invaluable aids to the broadcaster—probably more than in any other sport. Included in that release material are numerical rosters that are useful for quickly identifying players during a game, and three-deep depth charts, which supply by position each team's starters and reserves. It is from the "three-deeps" that broadcasters make up those vital spotting charts from which they work during a game.

I try to make up my spotting charts as early as possible and study them so thoroughly that by game day I know them as well as I know my address or phone number. That's my homework, and if I've done it properly it will usually pay off with a smooth broadcast. Sometimes, though, even all the preparation in the world won't carry you. There was, for example, the first football game I ever broadcast professionally. It was an absolute nightmare.

I was working for Marty Glickman at CBS at the time, and he was doing high school football throughout the New York metropolitan area. That, by the way, is the toughest kind of assignment because all of the youngsters are unfamiliar and you can't arm yourself with the kind of background material that can help you through a broadcast. Marty is a master at the task.

Because Glickman had an assignment conflict, I drew the job of covering a high school game for WJRZ, a Newark, New Jersey, radio station. It was a Thanksgiving Day game between two traditional opponents, and I went through all of the preparation I thought necessary. I talked to the two coaches. I watched the teams practice in the week before the game. I made up spotting charts the same way I would if it was the Dallas Cowboys playing the Oakland Raiders.

The result was an absolute, unqualified disaster. I have never had a worse time working at any event, and I'm sure it showed. Nothing seemed to go right, and I knew I was in trouble right from the start when I realized that the lineup numbers I had in front of me and the uniform numbers the players were wearing did not correspond. They had pulled a last-minute switch, leaving this very nervous freshman announcer in a pickle.

With a professional broadcaster, the commentary flows comfortably. In my first play-by-play job in the New York area, instead of flowing, I found myself with dead air—nothing to say. I produced an unsure "uh . . . uh," a couple of times.

A football game lasts something under three hours, but this one felt like an eternity. It seemed like we'd never get to halftime, and once we did it felt like the second half would go on forever. The longer it went, the worse things became. I felt like I was dying. I just wanted to close up and leave. Finally, mercifully, the clock ran down and this endless torture was brought to a bloodless conclusion. When we wrapped it up, the engineer turned to me and said, "Nice job." I laughed at the crack. I had been terrible and I knew it.

Marty Glickman had heard part of the broadcast and made some suggestions. To him, it wasn't as atrocious as I thought. His first suggestion was that I go right back at it. I'm glad I did. If I hadn't, and had chosen instead to brood over my disastrous debut, I would have been beaten. Instead, I began doing a high school series for a small Long Island station and that helped solve the problem. The more games I did, the more comfortable I felt with the broadcasts. But I will never forget that first one. There is no way I could.

I remember when I left that game, I felt terrible. The only thing that cheered me up was the realization that there weren't that many listeners to hear me. Ball players have bad games. I had a bad broadcast. Even now, if I have a lackluster performance, I'll go out into the street and look at all the people who are walking around—people who weren't home and didn't see or hear the show. That's always a good feeling—to know the whole world isn't watching or listening.

Sometimes a bad broadcast isn't the fault of the announcer—especially in football. That's because booth locations in some stadiums often leave much to be desired. There is, for example, Yale Bowl in New Haven, which the New York Giants called home for a few years while their magnificent new stadium was being constructed in East Rutherford, New Jersey. My fondest memory of the Yale Bowl was the day I had to do play-by-play while ducking snowballs from the fans. Sam Huff, the great Giant linebacker of the 1950s and 60s, was doing color on the radio broadcasts at that time, and one of the snowballs almost hit him. He said something sarcastic about it on the air, but what he didn't know was that some of the fans doing the throwing were also listening to the game on transistor radios. So Sam's remark produced a predictable follow-up. I still wince when I think about it.

Yale Bowl's broadcast facilities are a bit more spartan than most stadiums, but there are other places that aren't exactly ideal either. The Los Angeles Coliseum, which has a track running around the field, Soldiers Field in Chicago, New York's Shea Stadium, and Metropolitan Stadium in Bloomington, Minnesota are some of the less convenient places that I've worked in. On the other hand newer stadiums like Arrowhead in Kansas City, Giants Stadium, Rich Stadium in Buffalo, Three Rivers Stadium in Pittsburgh, and the New Orleans Superdome all are excellent to work in. You shouldn't let facilities affect your broadcast, but if you must work from a bad location, you may miss certain things. There isn't much you can do about that except hope you can get some help from a television replay.

Sometimes you can't believe what that instant replay shows. Imagine, for example, trying to describe Roy Riegels' gallop in the wrong direction during the Rose Bowl in 1929. I'm not sure how you'd handle that one. Lindsey Nelson had a similar dilemma during the Cotton Bowl game on January 1, 1954, when Alabama played Rice and Tommy Lewis jumped off the 'Bama bench to tackle Dickie Moegle, interrupting a certain touchdown run. That's a once-in-a-lifetime item, and Lindsey will never forget the small slice of college football history that he watched that day.

Ironically, the night before the game Nelson was going over the rule book with the immortal Red Grange, who was doing the color for the Cotton Bowl classic. And, quite coincidentally, he had mentioned the rule that permits the referee to award a

Lindsey Nelson (he's with Red Grange) saw his homework pay off. (NBC)

touchdown if a runner is tackled by a player coming off the bench. So he was familiar with the ruling, but he honestly never expected to have to use that knowledge the very next day.

"Moegle was running free," Nelson recalled. "He was going down the sidelines with only one Alabama player to beat, and that was a big tackle who had a long way to go and was coming from a bad angle. He was completely in the clear and in the next instant he was down at the 38-yard line and the run was over."

It had happened so quickly that even Nelson wasn't sure what he had seen. For an instant, the sickening thought crossed his mind that Moegle might have been shot. Then he saw Lewis, moving almost like a ghostlike creature, away from the fallen Rice player. And he began to realize what had happened—that a twelfth man had made the illegal tackle. Immediately, Nelson recalled his rules conversation with Grange the previous night, and confidently plunged ahead. "The rule clearly states that if a play is interfered with by an act palpably unfair, such as a twelfth man coming off the bench . . . the referee has the power to award a touchdown."

That, of course, is exactly what had happened, and when it did, Lindsey looked like a genius. That's because he had the good sense to prepare himself with a review of the rules, which made him ready for every contingency, even the rarely seen twelfth man tackler.

The rule book is a broadcaster's textbook. He's got to know it as well as the umpire or referee does. I'm not saying you should read the rules before every game, but a routine review now and then doesn't hurt. It's part of the announcer's homework. If you ignore that part of your professional responsibility you're liable to wind up the way one well-known broadcaster did when describing a long run from scrimmage.

". . . He's through the line and on his way," the announcer reported. ". . .He's at the 30 . . . the 35 . . . the 40 . . . the 45 . . . the 50 . . . the 55 . . . "

Bill Bradley was a Knick rookie in 1968 when I interviewed him. I wasn't exactly a veteran either. (GEORGE KALINSKY)

# 6 INTERVIEWING IS A TWO-WAY STREET

Once upon a time, when sportscasting was still in its dark ages, all you had to do was give the scores. Thirty seconds of who won and who lost and you were through. That was in the days when newspapermen never went to dressing rooms. They would watch the game and report what happened, rarely including the athlete's explanation or point of view.

That old-fashioned, lazy-man's journalism went out the window many years ago. Now the newspaper reader or television viewer wants to know more about individual athletes. Just who are these people and what makes them tick? It is the job of the sports writer or broadcaster to deliver that information, and the method is the sports interview, which gives some depth to the personalities who dominate the fun and games that occupy our time.

In this chapter we'll talk about the technique of interviewing an athlete, the questions that must be asked, and how to duck when the guy you're interviewing decides he doesn't like the direction of the conversation. Don't laugh. That's happened to every interviewer at least once and, more often than not, it is a weapon used by the subject to sidestep a tough question. When he starts getting abrasive, you know you've touched a tender spot. It doesn't mean there's anything wrong with the question. In fact, it means the question is probably a pretty good one.

The first thing to remember when you're interviewing anybody, whether your subject is an athlete or a public figure, is that you're representing your audience. That's why you ask questions—to get the answers the audience can't get for itself.

Really, you're just a middleman, bridging the gap between the public and your interview subject.

To conduct a sensible, significant interview, you must ask sensible, significant questions. There's no need to be abrasive, though. The important thing to keep in mind is that you must ask the questions that need to be asked. And if they're tough questions, well, that's the way it goes. Some athletes can handle the toughies with ease. Others aren't equipped to deal with anything more probing than, "How'd it feel to hit that home run?"

Athletes develop reputations with writers and broadcasters, and you learn quickly who the easy interviews are and who the tough ones are. One of the most pleasant talkers in sports has always been Tom Seaver. New York baseball writers were delighted when Reggie Jackson came to the Yankees because he always was a good interview. They learned fast about his other side. In basketball, Julius Erving is a pleasure to interview, but Kareem Abdul-Jabbar has a reputation as a toughie. In hockey, Rod Gilbert was always an excellent interview, but Bobby Orr was a tough nut to crack. It all depends, I guess, on the individual and his moods. Some people are outgoing and others aren't. Interviewing an affable guy is easy. It's interviewing the others that is a challenge.

Sports is like any other business. There are charming, interesting athletes and there are boorish, unpleasant ones. If you could choose, you'd concentrate on the first category. But you can't and so sometimes you must become involved with the second one. That's how I happened to bump heads with tennis champion Jimmy Connors.

Connors is rated as America's No. 1 men's tennis player. But he ranks somewhat lower than that when it comes to manners and behavior. Maybe he thinks that because he is a star he doesn't have to bother with simple basics such as courtesy. But his high-handed act loses more fans than it wins for him. People generally are turned off by wise guys and that's the image Connors generates. That act surfaces both on the court and off it and really it's just an outgrowth of what seems to be the excess supply of immaturity from which Jimmy suffers.

Some athletes would have you believe that they are doing you a tremendous favor in submitting to an interview, taking time out of their busy schedules to chat with you for a couple of minutes. It's ironic, really, because many of those interviews are arranged by press agents anxious to get their client before the public. The theory is that the public will get excited about the athlete and the event in which he is appearing and buy tickets. The key word here is "buy."

Connors was in New York to play in the Colgate Masters Grand Prix Tennis tournament, an event that claimed it would settle, once and for all, the question of who was No. 1 in men's tennis. It was a burning question because the crown was being claimed by a number of players including Connors and the man who had beaten him at Forest Hills four months earlier, Guillermo Vilas of Argentina. Vilas was the overwhelming crowd favorite in that tournament, the United States Open, a fact Connors can probably trace to his abrasive personality. After the match was over and Vilas had won, Connors pushed his way through the crowd, ignoring the post-match traditions in which losers always participate. Vilas hardly noticed, but the knowledgeable tennis fans did and gave Connors low marks for the rather unsportsmanlike performance.

The Masters Grand Prix was Connors' first appearance in New York since the United States Open incident, and the tournament was to be held in Madison Square Garden. The press people were hard at work in the days before action began, arranging interviews with the various players. High on the agenda of writers and broadcasters was the controversial Connors.

My interview with Mr. Tennis was set up and I arrived with a tape crew, intending to do a couple of minutes for both the 6 o'clock and 11 o'clock newscasts. We wound up running the entire piece on both shows, although it wasn't exactly what we might have expected when we logged in "Connors Interview," as part of the script.

Connors seemed annoyed when we started our conversation, acting as if he'd rather be someplace else. And things just deteriorated from there. It began this way:

Albert: "Jimmy, the last time you played in New York you were booed by the fans who rooted for Guillermo Vilas to beat you at Forest Hills. Do you think the same thing will happen in the Masters?"

Connors: "How should I know? You'd have to ask New Yorkers. What kind of question is that anyway? You're a New Yorker. Ask yourself."

Connors' snappy answer was totally in character for him, but

I wasn't in the mood for his churlish routine. Then he got playful, trying to soften the confrontation. He said, "Let me ask the questions," and with that took the microphone. "How do you think the crowd will react?" he asked me.

I decided to play along. "I don't think they'll react very well," I said. I guess that didn't sit well with Connors because he snapped back. "I don't react well to you." I tried to stay cool. "You asked the question and I gave you an honest answer," I said. By now Connors was steaming.

"I'll talk about the tournament but not an individual player like Vilas," he said. "But he's in the tournament," I replied. "Would you like to supply my questions?" That ended the interview. "I don't want to talk to you," Connors sputtered and stalked off.

I used the full spot, from start to finish, on both the early and the late sports shows. To me, the Connors' noninterview was like theater, and although it was certainly anything but the traditional sports interview, it did fulfill the requirement of providing insight into the subject. In Connors' case, in fact, it may have provided too much insight.

The Connors spot ignited a flood of reaction. His fans complained that I had embarrassed him. Other viewers said I should have belted him. I must admit that he managed to get my adrenalin flowing. Fortunately, most sports interviews are more peaceful than that.

I was more or less prepared for Connors' act because I know what kind of guy he is. And that's a very important part of the sports interview. You have to know your subject and that goes right back to doing your homework. Before you interview anybody, you should do a little research. In that way you can plan your questions and move the interview in the direction you want it to take. Carefully thought-out questions usually produce more meaningful responses. And that leads to a better interview.

It would be nice if you could outline every interview in advance. That would be ideal. But sometimes it doesn't work out that way. Suppose, for example, you go to an event with one subject in mind for an interview. When you get there you find that a retired ex-star who's rarely available has shown up that day. The logical thing to do is abandon your original subject and go for the guy who isn't available every day.

There is an important difference between interviews conducted by sports writers and the ones that sportscasters conduct. Usually, newsmen will gather around a player in a group of six or eight. A writer might ask one question in that setting and then just listen to the give-and-take as the conversation between the player and the other reporters continues. But the broadcaster must go one-on-one with his subject. He can't depend on colleagues to ask the interesting questions. He has to come up with them himself. That's why it's important for a broadcaster to do thorough preparation. I find the best way to do that is by reading. I study box scores to get a feeling of how individuals are doing and that way when it's time for me to go one-on-one, I'm ready.

An interview is a two-way street. So it's important that the person you're talking to be at ease. Some people simply freeze at the sight of a microphone. You have to work at relaxing them, sometimes with easy conversation before the formal interview begins. It can help if you tell the subject in general terms the direction your questions will take. He feels prepared when he has an idea of what's coming and that works in your behalf if it takes the fright of that mike out of him. When your subject is uptight about the interview, it comes across to the audience and can destroy the conversation.

Another method commonly used to calm a subject is to discuss something he is familiar with, things he's interested in

My subjects are a couple of Oakland A's after the 1974 World Series—Rollie Fingers on the right and Joe Rudi. (NBC)

and can discuss intelligently. Get him going on familiar ground, and he'll feel comfortable. It will show in the interview.

One of the things that worries athletes who agree to an interview is that a broadcaster will show them up. Some of them don't handle the language as well as they'd like and know it. The trick is to gain their confidence, convince them that you're not interested in anything more or less than a conversation that will give their fans a better idea of who they are and what they're all about. And really, that's the only legitimate reason for an interview—to add to the routine coverage of an event, to provide another dimension that can explain what's happened in the words of the person most directly involved, the athlete.

Sometimes you interview others involved in sports besides athletes. There are managers and coaches, front office people, and other executives. You have to deal with those types a little differently. They are the decision-makers, the people who are pulling the strings in sports. So you're asking different questions than you would be with an athlete. Sometimes the answers can be enormously interesting, or very boring. Perhaps the greatest interview subject in the history of sports was baseball hall of famer Casey Stengel, who communicated in his own special language, which in part depended on quick turns in direction and fractured syntax called Stengelese.

When you talked to Stengel, the question never really mattered because his answer was guaranteed to go off in a half dozen different directions. Ask Stengel why Ed Lopat, one of his pitchers, had so much success with his soft array of deliveries, and Casey would begin by telling you about Kirby Higbe, who had a herky-jerky delivery like Lopat's. Then you might get a short lecture on the old Brooklyn Dodgers, a team Higbe pitched for at one point. From there the conversation might make a quick turn to Leo Durocher, the longtime Dodger manager, and then, of course, to the "Gashouse Gang" St. Louis Cardinals, for whom Durocher once played. Meanwhile you'd be standing there with your microphone, trying to remember what you had asked Casey in the first place. But that was really no problem because invariably, Stengel would wind up back where you had started and, sometimes, he'd even answer the question. If he did, it would almost spoil the interview. Many broadcasters preserved their tapes of talks with Stengel because they are classics. At the Hall of Fame in Cooperstown, New York, there is a Stengel exhibit that includes a tape of Casey just talking. It is a fascinating example of the kind of delightful interview he always provided.

Stengel had a knack for using broadcasters and newsmen to his advantage. He endeared himself to them and was always available. Put a microphone in front of his face and off he went. There are other managers who aren't nearly as cooperative as he was and, in fact, will use the press as a target to unite their teams. I know one guy who makes a point of showing up a writer or broadcaster in front of his team for the purpose of creating togetherness in his clubhouse. When ballplayers or managers begin getting snappy with me, I feel they should remember that I don't win or lose games for them. I haven't pitched a shutout or hit a home run yet, and I haven't scored a goal or stopped one, or made a basket or grabbed a rebound. An athlete's performance is squarely up to him, the product of his own abilities, and sounding off on a newsman is a pretty poor way to hide any inadequacies that may surface.

That works both ways, though. There is no need to belabor a point with a manager or player who has just lost a tough game. Common sense should guide the broadcaster, who must realize that people in sports have feelings just like the rest of the world. When I go into a losers' dressing room I try not to upset my interview subject. He's aggravated enough about losing. I won't harp on a point or push for an answer when he's obviously not in the mood to give one. Again, it's just a matter of common sense and knowing when you can pursue a question and when it's time to stage a strategic retreat.

Winners' dressing rooms, of course, are always easier. Winners love to talk and wave "Hi" to mom back home. You try to keep that stuff to a minimum and deal with the pertinent action of the game. Remember, you are in the dressing room as a representative of your audience, charged with the task of asking questions you think they'd want answered. If you keep that basic fact in mind the job will be a lot simpler.

There are obvious and important differences in interviews conducted on radio and those done with the television camera's eye peeking over your shoulder. Microphones make some athletes self-conscious, but the combination of microphone and camera can be devastating. Once again, it is the responsibility of the interviewer to put his subject at ease, regardless of the medium. It's harder on television, but it can be done using the same standard techniques. Be prepared, and prepare the person you're talking to so that he won't be flustered when you ask questions. It's also a good idea to use television to your advantage. As a visual medium, it offers the opportunity to show as well as talk about things with an athlete. For example, baseball fans always marveled at home run king Hank Aaron's "quick wrists," which enabled him to get around on a pitch so rapidly. And football people always talked about Joe Namath's fast release on a passing play. On radio you can talk about those attributes. On television, you can show them.

Unless you are in a studio setting such as the "Five Minutes" segment, which is used on NewsCenter4, the one-on-one television interview comes across a bit flat. I'd much rather run-in action film or tape of the subject and use the interview as a backdrop narration for that. Pictorially, there is so much you can add to the routine question-answer format.

Some athletes do a complete flip-flop during their careers as far as interviews are concerned. That's what happened to basketball star Walt Frazier. When he first came to New York he was one of the best interview subjects in town, an excellent talker. Then, in his last year or so with the Knicks, he went into his Garbo act. You know, "I want to be alone." I thought that was really foolish on his part because it was his outgoing personality and availability to the media that made him so popular in the first place. When he was going well he was always an honest, outgoing guy. In the glory years of the Knicks, he may have been their very best talker. But when things went sour, he blamed the New York media. He's smart enough to know that the exposure the New York media gave him contributed to his image. But he left town with a sour taste.

In college basketball one of my favorite interviewees is always Al McGuire, the longtime coach at Marquette, who retired after his team won the NCAA championship in 1977. McGuire learned his basketball on the sidewalks of New York, a pretty good classroom if you ask me. He has an entire vocabulary of basketball jargon—Marquette called them McGuirisms—to describe particular situations. During interviews you never know what he might say, but you can be sure it will be terrific.

When the Denver Broncos made it to the Super Bowl in 1978, one of my favorite interview subjects, Craig Morton, was their quarterback. It couldn't have happened to a better guy. During his difficult days in New York with the Giants, Morton was

I've known Willis Reed since he came to the Knicks as a rookie out of Grambling . . . through two NBA championships and his stint as a coach. (GEORGE KALINSKY)

always accessible, always pleasant, always a good interview. He took so much garbage from the fans and would get hammered every week, just about destroyed game after game. But he handled it so well that I'll always admire him.

On the other hand there's another Giant who was quite the opposite. I've always felt that running back Larry Csonka has been an arrogant, uncooperative guy who displayed a terrible attitude about doing interviews. It was almost as if he was doing you a favor to consent to an interview, especially when he first came to New York. Sometimes, he outright refused to do them, and to me that's absolutely incomprehensible.

I've always found Billy Martin to be the same way . . . arrogant and negative about being interviewed. He elects to challenge the questioner and that's so unnecessary. But I guess it's a conditioned response with him by now. He has that street-fighter image to fulfill and that's the way he does it. It's funny, though, because baseball's original "Brat" was Eddie Stanky, the Martin of his era, and he's always been an outstanding interview.

Stanky will always be remembered for his controversial slide into Phil Rizzuto during the 1951 World Series, when he kicked the ball out of Rizzuto's glove. Rizzuto has never quite gotten over that play, and he bristles whenever Stanky's name is mentioned. Eddie, of course, feels he was right, and will, for life, and enjoys that upper hand. One time when I was doing pregame Yankee broadcasts, I had the two of them on together, and they handled the confrontation in good humor.

My relationship with Stanky is kind of special. I interviewed him many times, and we became close, off the field. We write each other often, and he'll always remain one of the favorite people I've encountered in sports.

Stanky's recognition factor is somewhat reduced because, except for one whirlwind day when he was hired to manage the Texas Rangers and then quit after a single game, he has been isolated in college baseball. But that's one problem Muhammad Ali will never encounter. Ali may be the best-known sports personality in history. He is recognized all over the world. His ratings, whether for a fight or a guest spot, are always incredible.

Ali is the consummate showman. He always has a new twist for his audience. When he went into his shell before fighting Leon Spinks, I felt he was getting bored with his own act. But the public ate it up and continued to be attracted to Ali even after he lost the championship to Spinks.

Ali is smart and that's the key to his value as an interview subject. Rarely does he answer a question straight out. He'll turn it around, something like the way Casey Stengel used to do, and then go into his act. It's always very good. And so is Ali whenever you put a microphone in front of him.

Perhaps the most effective interview combining news and insight that I've ever done was with Ed Snider, president of the Philadelphia Flyers of the National Hockey League. The Flyers were playing a crack Soviet team that was making a tour of NHL cities. Suddenly, the Russians, objecting to what they considered to be rough hockey that bent the rules too far to suit them, walked off the ice. It had all the earmarks of an international incident, and no one knew quite what would happen, either to the remainder of the game or to the tenuous relations between the Russians and the West. It was a nervous time for all concerned, and we wound up with Snider, one of the key men in the situation, in our booth. It was all a matter of catching the right guy in the right place. We were just lucky.

Snider was emotional and excited. He was taking a hard line with the Russians, angry over their ploy, and the words spilled out of him. It was an important interview, made so by the circumstances surrounding it and the fact that it was on national television. When the Russians decided to come back, it relieved a touchy situation.

One of the important things to remember when you're conducting an interview is to listen to the answers to your questions. Sometimes the subject will say something that will trigger my next question. And believe me, sports people can sense when an interviewer is listening to them or just standing there, holding a microphone, and waiting to ask the next question. If you're interested in what your subject has to say, he'll be more cooperative and usually will produce a brighter, better interview. And, after all, that's the whole idea.

Interviewing technique is like anything else in broadcasting. It takes time and practice to perfect it. The first time you try it, you may be discouraged because it seems like you have no idea what to say. But if you work at it and listen to other broadcasters, you begin to get a feel for the way to conduct an interview. And after a couple of times, you'll find the questions flowing comfortably and so will the conversation.

The broadcast booth at Madison Square Garden is directly over the route the players take to and from the dressing room.

# 7 "KICK SAVE, AND A BEAUTY!"

**B**ecause ice is in short supply in the temperate climate of Brooklyn, N. Y., I played my hockey on roller skates, and I can tell you that street hockey develops all the same emotions and excitement of that played on ice. It doesn't matter that you're skating on concrete instead of ice. And it was in those many games of street hockey that I developed my feeling for the sport.

I really believe that a broadcaster cannot comment on a sport adequately unless he has that understanding and feeling for it. If he doesn't, the delivery comes across as artificial and wooden. Having participated in the sport being described gives the announcer an extra dimension. That's why people like Phil Rizzuto in baseball and John Brodie and Len Dawson in football are so effective, and it explains why more and more stations and teams are seeking ex-players to go into broadcasting.

I got my fill of hockey in the streets, but my brother Al never had enough of the sport. Ice was scarce, but Al always seemed to find some. He was a fanatical goaltender who wasn't happy unless he was stopping shots. At one point he wanted to go to school in Canada so that his hockey progress wouldn't be interfered with by the lighter schedules United States colleges play. He wound up at Ohio University, and after graduation even went to a Ranger training camp one year. He was sent out to the International League, which is a circuit of small midwestern cities where you can still maintain your amateur status even though it is a professional league. Frank St. Marseille and Stan Jonathan played in the IHL and Ted Garvin, who once coached at Detroit, did a lot of coaching in that league. Al was a backup goalie and almost got killed. Then he decided to

73

become the team's broadcaster, which was a wise move for him. It's a lot safer in the radio booth.

When I first reached the hockey broadcast booth at Madison Square Garden, I found myself trying to tell the listeners everything that was going on. In hockey, that's simply impossible, and the broadcaster must learn to be selective. Radio hockey in particular can be very difficult for the listener if you're giving him too much information. Really, you should be talking in terms of patterns rather than following every pass from stick to stick. It's tough to use that many words, since if you get too caught up in a particular sequence in hockey, you fall behind. So I try to minimize my wordage.

That's not to suggest that you deliberately leave out anything when you broadcast a hockey game. Rather, you simply edit your material mentally before delivering it. You decide what is vital for the listener to know and what is not. The thing that is tough is that your editing decisions must be made in a split second and cannot interrupt the flow of your play-by-play delivery.

You must remember that on radio you are the eyes of the listener. He depends upon you totally to know what is happening. The first thing you must do, just as in basketball, is set the boundaries of the action. Once you establish the geography of the ice, people will get used to that and depend on it for the location of the action. That is how you establish the consistency of call that is so vital to a broadcaster's credibility.

So we start with the obvious—the red line, the Chicago and Ranger blue lines for example, and the two goal lines. Then, there is the right of the goal, left of the goal, behind the goal, far and near boards (from the broadcast location), center ice, Chicago's end and New York's end. Now you have some reference points on the ice that you can use to report the progress of the puck.

With the geography of the ice it's easier for a broadcaster to deliver the flow of play. For example, a typical Ranger play-by-play sequence might go something like this:

. . . *The Rangers start out of their own end. Esposito is to center. Right wing pass to Murdoch. He's across the line. Broken up by Chicago. Recovered. Back to Esposito . . .*

I think people listening to that would have a better picture of what was going on than if I followed the puck from stick to stick. Isn't it more effective to say, "The Rangers start out of their own end," than it would be to report each and every pass in their zone? After all, those preliminary passes are nothing more than the start of the team's move up ice and that's what we've reported, with fewer words and names so as not to confuse the listener.

Once the puck reaches the offensive zone I feel the broadcaster should capture everything he can. The strategy of my play-by-play changes here. When a team is attacking I feel the broadcaster should give every pass. There are times when you can't, of course, and that's when you hear . . . "Off the scramble—score!" Then the crowd's roar takes over and gives you time to reconstruct the goal in your mind's eye and report it to your listeners.

You're always fighting for time against the speed of the game. That's why it's important to give as much information as you can in as few words as is necessary. But one place I avoid cutting my verbiage is on a shot. I feel it is always important to tell the listener how the shot was stopped. It's far more descriptive to say glove save, stick save, pad save, or arm save. The more information on a shot, the better. Then it's up to the color man, when you get to the stoppage of play, to discuss the play in more detail if it was a significant shot. My feeling about describing the goalie's stop helped me develop the hockey phrase that is frequently associated with me—"Kick save, and a beauty!" That has become to my hockey play-by-play what "Yesss!" is for me in basketball.

Just as I try to describe the save, I also try to give the type of shot, if I can. On a slap shot, there's always time for that. You might say: " . . . Out to the right point. He lines it up. Slap shot! . . . " Wrist shots get off so quickly that there is rarely time to say anything more than " . . . He shoots . . . " But if the goalie gloves the shot and holds on, I will use the stoppage in play to add detail, saying, " . . . good wrist shot from 30 feet out on the right side . . . " just so the listeners will know where the action is. It's a word-picture that I am painting.

I try to tell the listener who the players on the ice are as frequently as I can. It becomes an automatic thing, even with the constant line changes. I like to give the audience an idea that things are happening, even away from the puck. This is where a broadcaster's preparation is very important. Doing so many

Ranger games, I am obviously familiar with the forward lines and defensive pairings, and I know pretty much who's playing with whom. In the days when Rod Gilbert, Jean Ratelle, and Vic Hadfield formed the hottest line in the NHL, I only had to see one of them on the ice and I automatically knew that the other two were about to join him if they weren't already out there. That's harder to do with visiting teams, especially now when you see them so infrequently. So before the game I'll make it a point to talk to an official of the other team to gather background information on what the line combinations are like. That makes it a little easier to keep track of the players when they change nonstop.

I try to put a little extra in my broadcasts if I can. Running down as many of the skaters as I can is part of that. I also like to point out things beyond the obvious shots, saves, and goals. One of the most vital elements of a hockey player's game is forechecking—his ability to bottle up the other team in their own end. I decided a long time ago that if forechecking was so important to coaches and general managers it ought to be part of my broadcasts, too. So I like to include it this way: " . . . Vadnais, trying to get out, checked closely by Jarvis. Starts out to his right, hemmed in, cuts back . . . " At least it gives the listener the picture of the guy watching his opposition, preventing him from starting up ice.

Perhaps the biggest problem for a broadcaster doing hockey besides, of course, keeping up with the speed of the game, are the names. There are many Frenchmen playing this game, and names like Jocelyn Guevremont and Yvan Cournoyer are constant challenges. There was one NHL public-address man who never could handle the problem. So when the Montreal Canadiens came to town, Jean Beliveau's last name would come out fine, but he would have to live for that night with "Gene" for his first name. And Henri Richard was always "Henry" instead of the proper "En-Ree." Proper pronunciation of names should be basic for any broadcaster. I don't care how tough they are. Butchering them over the air is like a newspaperman misspelling them in print.

Some names are easily pronounced but can cause other problems. Consider, for example, Don Luce of the Buffalo Sabres. The natural and logical play-by-play sequence might include: " . . . Luce in the corner . . . " But how do you differentiate between that and the frequently used " . . . loose in the corner . . . " The answer, of course, is to avoid the description "loose," when you're doing a Sabres game. But that means altering your normal delivery, and it is not easy to do.

Then there are defensemen Rick Lapointe of the Philadelphia Flyers and Guy Lapointe of the Montreal Canadiens. Both of them are regulars on the power play and often go out to play—you guessed it—the point. So it sometimes comes out " . . . at the point Lapointe . . . " or " . . . Lapointe, right point . . . " There's really nothing you can do about that unless you want to identify the place on the ice as the blue line. But that's really cheating the listener because "the point" is a much more specific spot on the ice and zeroes in on the action more precisely than "the blue line."

Most announcers are inconsistent about first names. There are sequences such as at the start of a game or the start of a period when I will use first names as often as possible. When you're starting a game, I feel it's more dramatic and also supplies the listener with more information which, after all, is your first priority. So I might begin the play-by-play call this way:

*It's Doug Jarvis lining up against Jean Ratelle. Jarvis with Doug Riseborough on this side and Mario Tremblay against Ratelle, Don Marcotte, and Terry O'Reilly.*

Even on changes, when you're hurrying to keep up with the action, it's a good idea to use first names when new skaters hit the ice. That's really newspaper style and, I think, just part of good basic reporting.

First names also can be helpful when you're doing teams with sets of brothers such as Denis and Jean Potvin of the New York Islanders. You have to identify which Potvin has the puck, and you also have to vary your method for separating them. So one time I might do it: " . . . There's Potvin, out of his own end. That's Denis. Over to brother Jean . . . " and another time, the delivery might be: " . . Denis Potvin carries up. Passes to Jean . . . " Sometimes I might do it this way: " . . . Denis Potvin passes to Nystrom . . . " But that form always sounds funny to me because my ear tells me that when I use one player's first name, I should also use the first name of the other. That's just an individual hangup, though.

The great thing about all sports, I think, are the names and the

Getting it straight from the Philadelphia Flyers' Bob Dailey.

drama you can build into some of them simply through the way you say them. It's the inflection and the way you break down a name. That's another reason for using a first name as frequently as possible. Instead of Jackson, or even Reggie Jackson, it's Reg-gie Jack-son. Adding the first name gives the announcer more to say and allows the name and the image of the player to linger with the listener. The syllabic pause, used properly, adds to the drama. You can do it with almost any name.

Much of the success of any hockey broadcast depends upon timing. With experience you learn just what your margin is between stoppages of play and how much you can get in without letting the game get away from you. In hockey sometimes the action begins almost as soon as the national anthem ends. It depends on the referee and how fast he drops the puck. I can sense the start coming as the referee moves toward the circle, and I have to judge how much time I have before the game begins. Certainly, I would want to identify the starting goaltenders, although that is often taken care of at the beginning of a broadcast, before the anthem. As play is beginning, I might say, " . . . Ken Dryden in the goal to our right and John Davidson to our left . . . "

The ideal beginning would be to identify the starting lineups for both teams. If there is no time for that I will try to at least name the two centers. That, after all, is where the action begins, so our audience should know at least who the two players on the faceoff are.

When you get right down to basics you must remember that basketball is an American sport and hockey is not. And that means that your average audience will be more familiar with basketball players than they are with hockey players. That's especially true when you're dealing with telecasts. When you're doing a radio broadcast, the audience consists of fans who are really into the sport. They're probably going to be familiar with the players except for brand-new rookies. With television, though, you get a more casual audience, perhaps dial-turners who've tuned to your station for a moment. So I feel I have to make my broadcast appeal to that kind of audience as much as to the fan who is totally familiar with the game.

The main difference between hockey and basketball on television is that you have to mention so much more with hockey. I feel the game is so fast, and the people don't know the players as well as they do in basketball. Therefore, there's more work for the announcer. I try not to say obvious things that are apparent visually, but occasionally things like "near boards" or "far boards," will slip through. I do believe in saying " . . . over the Ranger blue line . . . " because the perspective on television doesn't always allow the viewer to know which line the play is passing over. I don't think that's a bad thing to mention.

In televised basketball you might only identify the players by name as the ball moves from one man to another. In televised hockey there's more to report, more to explain to the viewer. Still, though, the broadcaster must limit himself and be careful not to broadcast the obvious. Here is a sequence from a Rangers-Montreal game presented first as I would broadcast it on radio and then as I would on television.

*. . . Off the faceoff, comes back to Vadnais at the blue line. Goes cross ice to Greschner at the near boards. Carries up to center. Poke checked away by Lafleur. Recovered by Vadnais.*

*Right wing pass to Hedberg at the Montreal blue line. Winds up*
*. . . shoots . . . deflected to the left. Savard gets to it and clears to*
*center . . .*

*. . . Carol Vadnais controls. To Greschner. Up for Hedberg.*
*Broken up by Lafleur. Vadnais. To Hedberg again. Shot.*
*Deflected. Savard clears . . .*

On TV the viewer sees the faceoff, so the broadcaster can
eliminate that detail. He sees the cross-ice pass. What the
play-by-play man must do is report who has the puck. There's
no need for "winds up." It's obvious. I would include the
deflection on TV, though, because sometimes the viewer can't
see that.

Essentially, a TV broadcast is more succinct. You are an
edited version of radio play-by-play and that makes the job
more difficult. You have to exercise control in this medium that
is not necessary on radio.

Like any other sport the best way to develop a good delivery
for broadcasting hockey is by doing it firsthand. There are a
number of ways to do this, but one of the most effective is to turn
down the TV sound and "broadcast" into a tape recorder. Play
back your tapes and try to analyze your performance. Did you
deliver the excitement of the game? Were you accurate? Did
you provide your listeners with all the information they needed?
Don't be afraid to be too critical of yourself. That's how you
improve.

Try to develop techniques that will enable you to cope with
the speed of the game. Don't depend on uniform numbers to
identify players. Try to pick up traits. Does a particular player
wear a helmet? Is he a left-handed shooter or right-handed? Is he
a fluid skater or does he lumber up and down the ice? Use
everything available to you to make your job easier. With
hockey's speed, a broadcaster needs every edge he can get to be
able to keep control of his delivery.

Hockey people used to think only Canadians could play their
game because Americans didn't get enough ice time. And there
are a lot of Canadians who think that Americans don't know
enough about their game to write or broadcast it. They just will
not accept an American reporting hockey. It's a ridiculous
situation. Look around the National Hockey League and you
see more and more United States–bred players. And most of the

broadcasters in the league are Americans. No matter how good a job they do, though, the Canadians seem to criticize.

As a kid I grew up listening to the broadcasts of Danny Gallivan from the Montreal Forum, and he captured the excitement of those great Canadian teams. He was a Canadian whom I respected.

Now I go to Canada and listen to some of their announcers, and I can tell you they just would not make it in the United States. It's a completely different style of broadcasting, but they're used to it and that's fine. What difference is there between Montreal and Minnesota? Those people who report on hockey in this country are every bit as competent and understand the game every bit as well as do the Canadians. After all, a hip check is a hip check, no matter which side of the border you're on.

Don Dunphy is at the Mutual microphone as Joe Louis has his hand aloft following his knockout of Billy Conn in 1941.
(DON DUNPHY COLLECTION)

# 8 AT HOME IN ANY SPORT

The men who are the true professionals in broadcasting are equally at home on any assignment. People like Lindsey Nelson, Vin Scully, Curt Gowdy and others have handled a variety of events during their careers. And in today's marketplace a broadcaster can't afford to limit himself to a single sport. Remember, the more versatile you are, the more you increase your job opportunities.

Each sport is different in its demands on a broadcaster. Baseball has the dead-air gaps to fill between pitches. Hockey and basketball are nonstop speed sports that make it difficult to stay with the action because it happens so fast. Football is a technical sport with a tangle of bodies to unravel on every play.

Then there are the other sports, where the action is dominated by a single or a couple of competitors rather than a team. Sports like boxing, horse racing, golf, and tennis have gained widespread exposure on radio and television. Track and field and soccer, although not covered quite as extensively, also have loyal followings. Each of those sports has developed its own legion of expert broadcasters as well—voices that are automatically identified with their sports. And, like the popular team sports, there is a technique that must be mastered for these events as well. Some of the experts like Don Dunphy in boxing and Marty Glickman in track and field developed styles so unique that their voices are unmistakable. Others, like racing's Dave Johnson, double as electronic broadcasters as well as public-address voices. Jim Simpson in golf and Tony Trabert and Bud Collins in tennis capture for the listener sports in which many fans now participate themselves.

One thing these specialists share with team sports broadcasters is their preparation before an event. Even though they qualify as experts in the particular field, preparation remains a major part of their jobs.

## TENNIS

"We do our homework," says Trabert, who prepped for his tennis broadcasts by being a world class player for many years and later as captain of the United States Davis Cup team. "We always try to have as much information about the tournament, the facility, the health of the players, prize money and whatever else we can put our hands on. We usually have 10 times the amount of information that we can ever use."

The man who is acknowledged as a veritable encyclopedia of tennis information is Collins, one of the most popular broadcasters around. He kiddingly refers to himself as "a tennis degenerate," but yields to no one on his knowledge of the game. And he readily displays the information in his broadcasts.

"I try to inform and entertain," he once said in *Sports Illustrated*. "Sports is supposed to be fun, and the sun will still come up after somebody loses. Sometimes I show off, sure, but I like to have fun with it. I find out what I want to know about the players, and I share that with the people. I think of myself as conversing with friends, and conversation should be both amusing and interesting. Everyone talks too much on TV, myself included, but I'm trying to keep it to a minimum. Tennis coverage can become even quieter as the public learns more about the sport."

Trabert, as you might expect from one so deeply involved for so long with the competitive aspects of the game, brings a no-nonsense approach to his tennis broadcasts.

"Interest in the game has grown so rapidly that the audience ranges from beginners to intermediate to advanced players," he explains. "I try to say something that is of interest to them all, be it racquet preparation, the importance of hitting the ball deep, and why, or what have you. I try to help the viewers with tactics, help them think along with the players. I think you can do a little subtle teaching, but I try not to simplify it too much."

Since tennis, like golf, is an individual game and since it gets most of its exposure on networks, new announcers sometimes have a problem dealing with tactics. Collins avoids the trap with detours constructed around tennis humor, often directed at himself. Trabert relies on his identification as an expert in the sport.

"When somebody says 'great return,' I often say, 'No, poor approach,' and then try to point out the difference and show, for example, why a guy would get passed on a shot," says Trabert. "I try to say something that will relate to the weekend players. If you make it too complicated, you lose the beginner and if you make it too simple, you lose the advanced players. What you try for is a middle ground."

In tennis the broadcaster doesn't always have a lot of time in which to be flip, although Collins, "the tennis maven," seems to find moments to include some offbeat comments, just to keep everybody loose.

"There isn't that much talking done on a tennis telecast," says Trabert, "because we make an effort not to talk while the ball is in play. When a ball goes out, they have ballboys who toss them another ball and away they go. There isn't that much time between points, either, and when they change ends, there is, inevitably, a commercial. It's not like a guy throwing a 50-yard bomb and then the receiver walks back to the huddle, and you have a minute and a half or two minutes while they huddle and talk it over. We have to be concise. You can't get into long, rambling dissertations."

Tennis is unique in that much of the coverage seen on television is taped. Trabert, however, prefers live coverage of the events he's working on.

"When you tape, they have to edit it down to fit the time slot, and you often lose a piece of information," he says. "That happened to me once on a doubles match I was handling. I was describing the Australian doubles formation and why this particular team had gone into it, how it works, and how you attack it. The doubles team pulled out of it for a while and then, about four minutes later, went back into the formation. When the tape was shown, the first segment was edited out but the second appeared intact. So did my commentary which said, 'Here they go into the Australian doubles formation, again,' but, of course, with the explanation edited out, the audience had to be wondering why we didn't tell them what it was."

That's show business.

## GOLF

Golf is like tennis in that so large a part of the audience participates in the sport firsthand and knows the intricacies of it. Sportscasters have to be careful here because they're talking to a pretty knowledgeable audience. Coverage of golf has increased and, at the same time, improved drastically in recent years. Some of the sport's pioneers remember the difficult, early times.

"I did many of the first golf tournaments, and we couldn't figure out what to do," says Lindsey Nelson. "We had no mobility. If we were told a guy was 3-under-par on the 15th coming out of the dogleg, we had to believe it. Sometimes it wasn't so. And, of course, you'd built your whole presentation on this fact."

Jim Simpson, who does many PGA events, can testify to the accuracy of Nelson's account—from first-hand experience.

"It was in 1956 in the National Open at Rochester, New York, which was won by Cary Middlecoff," says Simpson. "Ben Hogan had a shot at Middlecoff at the 18th hole and missed it. Doug Ford had a shot at him at 18 and didn't get it. Ted Krol had a shot at him at 16, which was my hole."

Simpson, working the first golf broadcast of his career, was being extra careful on the straightaway, par-four 16th hole. "Krol hit his first shot to his left, to my right, off the fairway. He then hit his second shot into the pines. He hit his third shot across the green into the trap on the other side. He hit his fourth shot back onto the green and then double-putted for a bogey six."

Simpson had watched the action carefully, added the shots and reported them dutifully. "I then gave it back to the broadcasters at 18 and as I came walking up the fairway, I heard an announcement.

" 'Here's a correction on that score at 16,' the announcer said. 'Krol took a seven, not a six.'

"It sent a shudder right through me," remembers Simpson. "It turned out that Krol had called the extra shot on himself. He had broken his wrists over the ball while in the pines, and I had no way of knowing it.

"The point is that you're at the mercy of the scores being correct. It happens a lot less now because communications are so much better. But because of the scope of its playing area, I've

Chris Schenkel can't be telling Arnold Palmer how to play his next shot. (ABC-TV)

always felt golf is the most difficult of all sports to telecast. You have courses that are 7,000 yards long and a man hits a ball down into the woods or the rough and you think it's the next shot from that point. But when you remember my experience with Krol at the 16th hole, you know you never can be sure.''

One of the things every golf broadcaster makes sure to do is walk the course. In that way you get to see each hole, and you won't be working in the dark when you try to describe it. Otherwise, you'll be doing the kind of re-creations I used to do on baseball, sitting in a studio, working "blind." While walking the course, you note the obstacles facing the golfers when they play each hole. Simpson's tour of the 18 holes includes a special piece of preparation. He steps off the distance from each pin.

"Let's say the pin is dead center on the green," explains Simpson. "I will pace off the distance from the front of the green to the pin. The same thing from the back and the sides. Let's say a player hits a shot that is halfway between the front of the green and the pin and it's 30 yards or 90 feet from the front of the green to the pin. I can say that he is 45 feet from the pin. I know what I'm talking about because I've paced it off."

Another complication for the broadcaster covering golf is the sheer distance from the players. You can recognize Jack Nicklaus if he's standing next to you or even 100 yards away. But when you're looking for him at a distance of 450 yards and he's surrounded by a gallery of people, well, it's almost impossible. So, the broadcaster takes note of what the golfers are wearing. It's much easier if you're looking for a blue shirt or white pants from that distance.

Just like tennis, there are times when golf broadcasting requires silence instead of commentary. The number one rule is that when a man addresses the ball, preparing for his shot, the announcer backs off and shuts up. Once a player starts measuring the shot, the announcer is as quiet as if he was playing the hole himself.

When he's working as an anchor man, removed from the individual hole action, Simpson avoids trapping himself with guesswork. "I never call a club," he says. "I never say, 'I think he's going to use a 5 or a 6,' on a particular shot. Now that we have people walking the course with the players, they can see and will tell us, 'he's using a 4 or a 5.' "

In a way, golf is very much like baseball. "The big question," says Simpson, "is how good are you when there is nothing going on? When you are doing hockey or basketball where there is continuous action, you just describe it. That's what you are trained to do; just keep up with the puck or the ball or whatever. In golf, when a man is walking 250 yards up the fairway, there isn't a whole lot of action to describe. So you have to be informative and entertaining. You have to keep the broadcast moving. You may have a winner at 14, but you have to sustain it through the next four holes and make it interesting. That's a challenge."

## HORSE RACING

Most sports broadcasters are dealing with human beings who are easily identified by the way they look. You'd never mistake Willie McCovey for Freddie Patek. Racing broadcasters, though, don't have that advantage. They're dealing with horses, which basically all look alike. They only means they have for separating them are the colored silks they carry, and that can be a tricky job when you've got six or eight horses bunched together, pounding down the backstretch.

Those who handle this assignment have one of the toughest jobs in this business. Complicating it is the fact that they often must handle the full slate of eight or nine races on a given day at the track, delivering the call for the fans at races, and then shifting gears for a broadcast audience.

The late Chick Anderson was the voice of the New York Racing Association. He delivered the call at Aqueduct, Belmont Park, and Saratoga, and he used to say that the race announcer not only must learn the horses for each race and have them committed to memory, but he must also be able to forget them just as quickly because as soon as one race is over, preparation begins for the next one.

"You have to memorize it just enough to get them (through the race) and then forget it," Anderson said. "Most people don't realize how difficult this really can be. It's a trick, a technique that some can do and others can't. Their minds simply aren't geared to it. You'd be surprised how easy it is to make a slip."

Anderson, knew firsthand. He confused Prince Thou Art for Foolish Pleasure in the 1975 Preakness. But those things happen. In the same race in 1947, Clem McCarthy, a pioneer in

Freddie Capossella was the dean of horse racing announcers.

the business, miscalled Jet Pilot for Faultless. So Anderson was in good company. And with as many as 480 individual memorizations to do each week, a mistake here and there is inevitable.

Like so many track announcers, Anderson did double duty, handling the call for the fans at the races as well as the broadcast audience. And he had a different style for each.

"The big difference is that for the track you are calling a race primarily for the bettors," he said. "So you minimize the entertainment aspect and concentrate on giving them accurate information. My intention is to give them useful information while they're watching so that they know where their horse is at any given time. I try to use phrases that locate the horses for them—inside, outside, between horses, trailing, and so forth. There are specific terms I use like 'trying to get through' or 'looking for room.'

"On television, of course, it is more of an entertainment call. A lot of the time I'll do simulcasts with the fans at the track getting the same call as those at home. But I aim that kind of call for the people sitting in their living room, just watching the race. I'll use fractional times, what the riders are doing and a lot of other information that I don't use normally. There's a considerable difference in the calls. The television call is a good deal more entertaining, I think, and it tends to get conversational. A track call is stylized and you do tend to call at more or less the same points (in the race) all the time."

Some racing announcers depend on the tradition of calling the horses at fixed positions on the track such as the three-quarter pole, the quarter pole, and so forth. Clem McCarthy and Fred Capossella, among others, favored that style. Anderson did not.

"I don't believe in it," he said. "I don't think people know what you're talking about. I try to use terms I think are more helpful like 'midway' or 'going into the turn.' "

Like their counterparts in golf, horse racing announcers are often well removed from the action. Often, because of the distance of a particular event, the race begins on the far side of the track, forcing the announcer to depend either on binoculars or, if the race is televised, a TV monitor.

"When a race starts on the other side of the track it can be a problem," Anderson said. "If they break well, you might have a horse on the inside, a horse on the outside, and another one in-between. You call a race by color identification, combining the stable silks with the names, or the other way around, and you may not be able to see well enough to be certain which horse is in-between. What I generally do is fake it one time, just go right over him and then go back to see which horse it is as quickly as I can."

Cawood Ledford, who calls the races for Louisville radio station WHAS, has the most enviable job in his business. Each year, on the first Saturday in May, he handles the call for the Kentucky Derby on network radio. Millions of people who pay no attention at all to horse racing the rest of the year are interested in the winner of the Derby, so Ledford has an enormous audience that comprises casual fans as well as devoted railbirds. He handles the assignment with a minimum of problems, thanks to proper preparation.

"On the morning of the race," Ledford told *Newsday* columnist Stan Isaacs, "I'll go to the jocks' quarters where the fellow who is in charge of the colors hangs all the Derby colors in one place. I look at the colors for a half hour, putting the name of the horse with each silk.

"A man on radio and television has to go with the developing story. I try to get all the way through the field as they go through the first turn, then, after that, go back to any horse that has a shot. If one of the favorites is trailing, I'll always go back to him, because he is always one you have to consider."

Ledford spends Derby week talking to the trainers and trying to learn how each horse will run the race. That way he can point out any strategy changes as the race is in progress.

"I am better prepared for a Derby than any other race," he says. "The problem is not to overthink the race. I'll be busy doing all the previous races on TV, so I won't have time to fret about it."

No matter how carefully an announcer prepares himself, mistakes happen. Fred Capossella, one of the deans of the profession, told author Maury Allen about a couple of his miscues in the book *Voices of Sport.*

"I once had a horse named Aching Back and I called him Aching Feet," said Capossella. "I had another horse named Nashville. For some reason, I kept calling him Louisville."

Capossella emphasizes the importance of being able to instantly forget the identifications it has taken the track announcer so long to memorize. "Five minutes after the race is over, I don't have the slightest idea who ran in it or who won," he said.

"I've done all kinds of sports," Chick Anderson concluded, "and I believe that calling a horse race must be the most difficult of any sport. I don't think anything else even comes close. It is the fastest. It requires you to work the greatest distance from the event, and it also requires you to memorize daily between 80 and 95 combinations of colors and names and then forget them immediately. You will have nearly 500 memorizations per week. Just let your mind wander for 15 seconds or so and you can call the wrong horse. Keeping each race straight is something that can't be done by everybody, just those of us who are crazy enough to go into this business."

## TRACK AND FIELD

Today, it's quite routine for athletes to move from the playing field to the broadcast booth. I guess the trend is most noticeable in baseball and football. But one of the first to make that difficult switch was Glickman, an outstanding track-and-field competitor. And he is probably the premier broadcaster of those events in this country.

Glickman was a member of the 1936 United States Olympic team that included the great Jesse Owens, and he began his sportscasting career in 1940 with the Millrose Games at Madison Square Garden after having competed in the same meet in each of the previous five years. Later, Marty branched out into other sports like basketball and football, but he has always felt a bit closer to track and field—the sport in which he was an Olympian. He is still deeply involved in it and, ironically, often must battle the same identification problems with human runners that horse race broadcasters have with the thoroughbreds.

"The most important thing about a track meet is the identification of the individual athlete," says Glickman. "There is no way you can identify track performers the way you can athletes in most other sports. They're seen so briefly, you've got to identify them immediately. You can't use a spotting chart the way you do in other sports—football, baseball, basketball, and the like."

This recognition problem is complicated by the fact that camera coverage shifts from one event to another quite quickly.

At a track meet, athletes are scattered all over the place, with three or four events going on at once. Marty says a broadcaster must be aware of those quick switches to avoid the pitfalls.

"You must know immediately who is competing in which events . . . who's up in the high jump or who's in the shot put circle. You'll switch from the mile to the pole vault or to the high jump. It's like a three-ring circus out there."

Like any good, professional broadcaster, Glickman studies his specialty. Having been a competitor in the sport helps, too.

"You have to know race tactics," he says. "If you know the individuals well enough to know if they have a great finishing kick or if they run four laps at an even pace, this is important information for a viewer. You have to know the event, what techniques are used. The geography of the situation is also important. When they are in the stretch, when they are in the turn, how many yards to go? You should tell the viewer how many laps to the mile, how many yards to the lap, and so on. Whatever the distance, you have to tell the viewer how close to the finish the runners are. You almost never see a runner and the finish line until the runner is, himself, at that finish line."

Glickman sees his role as more than just a flat-out, straightforward reporter who tells his listener which runner won the race. The nature of track-and-field events requires more than that from the broadcaster.

"You have to be able to aid the viewer," explains Marty. "You should tell them how to watch a race. For instance, when the runners start in staggered starting positions, you've got to explain that if the race was not run that way, the man on the inside would have a tremendous advantage because of the circular track. Let's say you're doing a 400-meter hurdle race from a staggered start. It's easy to tell who's leading—it's the first man over each hurdle who's in front. But in other events, you should say, 'Look for this . . . watch the man on the inside.' In a quarter, for instance, if the man on the outside is farther away from the man on the inside when they come out of the turn, then he is doing much better. Of course, when they straighten out, it's easy to tell who's ahead."

Like all sports, Glickman feels strongly that announcers should have a working knowledge of the history of track and field as well as insight into the thinking of the competitors.

"If you don't know the relative times, the history of the event, you can't put the athletes in perspective, and you have no business doing a track meet. Now, I'm also talking about the style and technique. The way a man runs may remind me of some other runner, and I'll say so. You establish your credibility with the viewer by your knowledge of the history of the sport. I use the general term knowledgeability here, too. If a racer runs the half in 2:04, then there is no chance for a four-minute mile. Just forget about it in your description. If you refer to it, your credibility is shot.

"On that point, I think that there is too much emphasis on time. Many men run to win and the time is not really paramount. I would not say that time is irrelevent. Certainly it is not because runners are always aware of time—time and distance. But too many writers and broadcasters talk about disappointing results because of the time. The idea is to win."

That's the same syndrome you sometimes see in other sports. When Ron Guidry, the pitcher for the New York Yankees, struck out 18 batters in one game, fans booed when Guidry got a hitter on a fly ball or a grounder. It was almost as if anything less than a strikeout was a failure. Well, it wasn't for him and it wouldn't be for a miler who wins his race, even though he doesn't break the four-minute barrier.

Glickman also feels that the track-and-field broadcaster should be able to do analysis as part of his commentary, since the color man in track events is generally confined to doing interviews in the infield instead of sitting in the broadcast booth, commenting while events are in progress.

"When a runner is beginning to tire, you should know that," says Marty. "The bobbing of the head, the forward lean, the arm action will tell you that; and, if he looks like he's running uphill, that will tell you, too."

## BOXING

Another sport where the announcer must be aware of telltale signs of weariness on the part of the participant is boxing. For me, and millions of others who've listened to his descriptions of scores of championship fights, the dean of boxing broadcasters is Don Dunphy, who spans the modern eras of the sport, from Joe Louis to Muhammad Ali.

Dunphy has been doing ringside, blow-by-blow commentary since 1941, and he follows the same regimen today that he did when he was first starting out. "I still go to the gym and watch the fighters work òut," he says. "I always did, and I think that's important."

At the start of his career, Dunphy did radio descriptions of the fights. The Friday Night Fights were a ritual for boxing fans, who hung on Dunphy's blow-by-blow accounts of some memorable bouts. Then came television and later closed-circuit and cable telecasts. Dunphy has worked in all three media.

"In radio, you are, of course, the eyes of the listening audience," he says. "In television, the camera is their eyes and a lot of television announcers make the mistake of telling the audience what it already can see. I say this: Radio is harder physically, but easier mentally. If you can describe an event, and I am fortunate in that I can describe one, you tell the audience just what you see. But doing three minutes of boxing maybe 10 or 15 times in a night is a physical event, and you have to condition yourself for it."

Dunphy actually trains for each assignment, without doing roadwork or punching the bag.

"You have to be in shape for it," he says. "If I'm asked to do a championship bout like Ali-Spinks, I have to assume that it will go the full 15 rounds. For the first Ali-Spinks fight, many of the people working the bout, myself included, thought it might be an early knockout. But I didn't take any chances and when it went the distance, I was prepared. I sit down with a stopwatch and train myself. You work up to fight night. It's like a baseball player in spring training. I will talk fast for three minutes, the length of a round, then rest for a minute, just like an athlete. When you're young, maybe you can get away with not taking care of your voice, but I think you're foolish if you don't care for it."

While boxing has time limits like most of the sports the rest of us deal with, it also has an element that most of us have to face only when we get into an overtime situation; the sudden ending. You can have as little as 10 seconds in which to tell the story. Dunphy is very conscious of that factor.

"Even on television, which is to me, very easy physically, there is a mental strain," he says. "You are thinking to yourself, 'Am I talking too much? Am I talking too little? Am I being trite?' But you have to be alert all the time. You can get into a long run of verbiage and suddenly see the man in front of you down on the floor. A man can go down very quickly from a knockout, and you have to be ready for that instant no matter what."

Another aspect of boxing that differs from other sports is the absence of a score. One man may be well ahead of the other and the announcer can say that, but there are no tangible points or numbers to which he can refer. So he must depend on his own knowledge of the sport to tell the story. Dunphy's first big assignment had exactly those circumstances.

It was the Joe Louis-Billy Conn heavyweight championship at New York's Polo Grounds on June 18, 1941. For 12 rounds, Conn was in front of the champion on points because of his clever boxing skills, Dunphy reported just what was happening—a major boxing upset with the heavyweight championship of the world looking very much like it would change hands. Suddenly, in round 13, Conn changed tactics and decided to turn slugger. Against Louis, it was a fatal mistake, and just that quickly, the challenger was on his back, being counted out as Louis retained his title. It was a trial by fire for a young boxing broadcaster making his debut in the major leagues of the fight game. Dunphy earned some battle stars that night for the sudden turnaround which he handled so coolly. And he's added more than a few to his collection since then.

## SOCCER

The newest big league action on the American sports horizon is soccer, which has built a large following in the United States over the last few years. Soccer is unique because it is played on running time without timeouts as such on a regular basis. That means nonstop broadcasting—a difficult assignment. A fairly new group of announcers has come along in recent years to handle soccer. Among the few American-born announcers in the sport are Jim Karvellas and Jon Miller. Miller has done play-by-play on both radio and television for two different teams in the North American Soccer League and was also the voice of the league's national network telecasts.

"The toughest thing about soccer telecasts or broadcasts for that matter is that you don't get a whole lot of publicity on the teams," says Miller. "And every time you do a game, you have to deal with a whole host of new players. In baseball or any other major sports you can follow the teams through the box scores in the newspapers. You can only do so much by memorizing names and numbers, and this is a problem with soccer. Of course, if you have seen the team before, you might remember that somebody has blond hair or long hair or whatever. But the real difficulty is that you don't know what these guys can do. You may know that he is a good goal scorer, but you don't know why. As a consequence, you can't educate your audience as much as you would like."

The absence of timeouts makes broadcasting soccer one of the most challenging jobs in our business.

"After a soccer game, I'm shot," says Miller. "I'm drained. Even in basketball, you get free throws and timeouts, but not in soccer. The big problem with that is getting the commercials in. Since you have continuous action, I try to pick the least offensive spot for a commercial and hope that we don't miss a goal. It's also very tough to work with a color man in soccer for this reason. He has to make his remarks not only meaningful, but succinct. It's not like football where you've got maybe thirty seconds to fill while the team is huddling for the next play."

Miller also tries to lead his listeners through the game by changing the inflection of his voice to reflect the action. Done properly, this is a key technique for all broadcasters.

"I found that a lot of times people will watch the game on television but don't see the situation developing. All they know is that the shot went 20 yards wide. What I try to do is build that up, giving them the feeling that something could happen before that thrust. I use an even monotone most of the time, then the voice gets a little shrill and, boom, here comes the shot. When I started doing national games, I worked on trying to get the anticipation so that the viewers know when the teams might get something going and have a scoring chance. You know the traditional network style, it's sort of a laid-back style, and I didn't feel it would work here. Maybe you had to over-talk. If you were born in Europe and grew up with the game, you might think that I am talking too much, but for the pople who are just tuning in to soccer, it works quite well. When the game itself is in progress, I try to generally place the ball within the geography of the field. I think it's more important to place the ball generally than it is to catch every pass."

Broadcasters like Dunphy, Glickman, Miller and the others share in common a singular goal. They're all on the job to capture the event for their viewers and listeners—to act as their pipeline to the action.

Ernie Harwell was the TV man when the New York Giants' Bobby Thomson hit his unforgettable homer against the Brooklyn Dodgers. (SCOTTY KILPATRICK)

# 9 MEMORABLE GAMES

It is, quite simply, the greatest play-by-play sequence in sports broadcasting and it lives on as a tribute to the late Russ Hodges, a pioneer in my business who captured the excitement and drama of Bobby Thomson's pennant-winning home run for the New York Giants against the Brooklyn Dodgers in the 1951 National League pennant playoff.

Hodges was working on the radio side when the Giants and Dodgers reached the ninth inning of the third and final playoff game. His broadcast partner, Ernie Harwell, who now works for the Detroit Tigers, was doing the telecast at the time and it is certainly no reflection on his considerable talent that few people can recall his report and that anybody who has ever been exposed to it can almost repeat Hodges' description, word for word. The nature of the medium makes radio a much more dramatic report. That's because the radio broadcaster is everything—eyes and ears and emotions—for the listener. He must capture the total feeling of the situation because the listener is depending upon him completely. On TV, the viewer can see what is happening and the broadcast is merely an added element. On radio, the broadcast is the *only* element.

Hodges and Harwell rotated from radio to TV and back just as current baseball broadcasters do. And it was just the luck of the draw that put Hodges in front of the microphone for that dramatic ninth inning. The Giants, trailing 4-1, had scored one run and had runners at second and third base with one out when Ralph Branca relieved Don Newcombe on the mound as Thomson stepped up to the plate. Here is how Hodges told what happened next:

The late Russ Hodges and Willie Mays were principals in the New York and San Francisco Giant legend. (KSFO)

*Bobby Thomson up there swinging. He's had two out of three, a single and a double. One out, last of the ninth. Bobby takes a called strike on the inside corner. Bobby hitting at .292. Brooklyn leads it, 4-2. Hartung down the line at third, not taking any chances. Lockman without too big a lead at second but he'll be running like the wind if Bobby hits one. There's a line drive . . . The Giants win the pennant . . . The Giants win the pennant . . . The Giants win the pennant . . . The Giants win the pennant . . . Bobby Thomson hits into the lower deck of the left field stands . . . They're going crazy . . . They're going crazy . . . Ohhh . . . Ohhh . . . I don't believe it . . . I don't believe it . . . I do not believe it . . .*

Hodges had broadcasting's most difficult job. The game, the pennant, the whole season had turned around on one swing of Thomson's bat. The Polo Grounds really did go crazy because of how suddenly it all had ended. And Hodges, as the Giants' broadcaster, was obviously caught up in the emotion of the moment. But his professionalism took over and he first delivered the news which, after all, was "The Giants win the pennant."

Hodges had a long and distinguished broadcasting career but nothing before or after approached the excitement and drama of that magic moment on October 3, 1951. It wasn't so magical for me, though, because I was growing up in Brooklyn, New York, so you know which team I was rooting for as an eight-year-old on that memorable day.

Rarely does a season in any sport come down to a climactic, final play the way the 1951 National League baseball race did.

But you don't have to run out the string quite that far to have memorable broadcasts, either. And I've had my share of them as well.

Part of Hodges' excitement on the Thomson broadcast was that the Giants were winning their first pennant in a long time. I can appreciate how he must have felt because I remember the emotions I felt when the New York Knickerbockers won their first National Basketball Association championship in 1970. Keep in mind that my association with the Knicks began as a ballboy, sitting under the basket. I waited a long time for that magic moment when the fans overran the court, howling, "We're Number One!"

The Knicks were born in 1946 as charter members of the Basketball Association of America, forerunner of today's NBA. Their fortunes were checkered, winning some years, losing in most, and rarely challenging for the championship. For 24 seasons, they drifted along with a revolving door of players memorable only to the fans who showed up regularly at Madison Square Garden (and occasionally at the dimly lit 69th Regiment Armory where the club played some home games) to cheer for New York's first modern pro basketball team.

For a long time they floundered, sabotaged by a combination of poor drafts and bad luck. In 1956, when Boston drafted Tom Heinsohn and K. C. Jones and traded for another first-round pick, Bill Russell, the Knicks selected Ronnie Shavlik as their Number One pick. In 1960, when the first round of the draft yielded people like Oscar Robertson, Jerry West, and Tom Sanders, the Knicks' pick was Darrall Imhoff. Now, Shavlik and Imhoff are both fine fellows, but neither fit into pro basketball nearly as well as some of the talent the Knicks passed up. In 1962, the draft's first round yielded people like John Havlicek, Jerry Lucas, Dave DeBusschere, Leroy Ellis, Zelmo Beaty, and Len Chappell. The Knicks' selection? Paul Hogue.

They began to turn the corner in 1964 when Eddie Donovan moved from the coach's job to become general manager of the team. That year, in the draft's second round, the Knicks drafted a six-foot-nine center from Grambling. Willis Reed would become the nucleus around which a championship was constructed. In 1965 the draft yielded Bill Bradley, who took a couple of years to study on a Rhodes scholarship before joining the NBA, and Dave Stallworth. In 1966 it was Cazzie Russell, and 1967 delivered Walt Frazier and Phil Jackson. Slowly the pieces of the puzzle were being constructed by Donovan and the new Knicks' coach, Red Holzman.

Holzman had been plucked out of his comfortable scouting job and dropped into the coaching pressure cooker. He brought with him a concept of team play and a defensive-oriented approach to the game that made the Knicks something special to watch. Reed was installed at center. DeBusschere, acquired from Detroit in a key trade, and Bradley, back from his Rhodes sojourn, were the forwards, with Frazier, drafted on the strength of a phenomenal performance in the National Invitation Tournament, and Dick Barnett, another trade acquisition, at the guards.

The tower of strength was the man in the middle. Reed was the captain of the team, a leader in every sense of the word and one of the best players at his position in the league. DeBusschere was the "power forward," a tremendous rebounder and one of the club's best defensive players. Bradley was the "small forward," the perfect front-court complement for Reed and DeBusschere. Barnett was the shooting guard with an outside jump shot he tabbed, "fall back, baby," because almost every time he threw it up, the ball would drop in for two points and it was time to fall back on defense. Frazier was the playmaker and defensive leader, with hands that could snap out at the ball with the speed of a snake's tongue. Together, they were the New York Knicks and 1969-70 was to be their year.

They won the first five games, lost one, and then set an NBA record with 18 consecutive victories, winning games in every way imaginable. They would jump in front and win. They would trade basket for basket and win. And they would fall behind and win. Perhaps the most memorable victory in that early season surge to the top was an unlikely Christmas night victory over Detroit. Trailing by one point with one second left on the clock, the Knicks called a timeout to get the ball at midcourt. They had only one chance—the old Alley-Oop play, with the guard throwing in the ball high and toward the basket and a teammate soaring to meet it at its apex and stuff it through. The problem with the maneuver is that everybody in the building, including the Pistons, knew it was coming. The element of surprise would not be involved.

Frazier stood at the side court and Detroit's Jimmy Walker left him alone, preferring to drop back and help on defense. Reed circled near the basket and in an instant Frazier fired the ball. As it neared the rim, Reed jumped to meet it. The timing had to be perfect and it was. The Knick center turned the ball through the basket and New York had a most unlikely victory. My voice cracked as I screamed into the microphone. Now I knew what Russ Hodges had gone through. But still more memories were ahead in that tremendous season.

In the playoffs the Knicks opened against Baltimore and eliminated the Bullets in a tough seven-game grind. Then came the semifinals against Milwaukee, with a giant rookie named Lew Alcindor who is now known as Kareem Abdul-Jabbar. Alcindor had lifted the Bucks from last place in 1968-69 to second place in his first NBA season. He had averaged 36 points per game in the first round of the playoffs as Milwaukee eliminated Philadelphia. But in the semifinals Reed controlled the big youngster, and the Knicks won in five games. Now it was on to the final series, the championship showdown against the Los Angeles Lakers.

Waiting for Reed this time was another giant, the Lakers' awesome Wilt Chamberlain. And the big guy had a couple of pretty good playmates in forward Elgin Baylor and guard Jerry West. That trio represents three of the finest players ever to perform in the NBA. And, going into the 1970 finals, Baylor, West, and Chamberlain stood 1-2-3 in career playoff scoring. The highest any Knick stood in playoff scoring was Dick Barnett's 17th, and most of that was accomplished with the Lakers.

It had been a difficult season for Chamberlain, who ruptured a tendon in his right kneecap and was sidelined for four and a half months. He had only returned to action in the final week of the regular season as the Lakers primed themselves for the playoffs. Los Angeles had reached the NBA finals seven times in the previous nine seasons and lost every one of them. The Lakers were becoming perfect bridesmaids, but this time they wanted to catch the bouquet.

The two teams split the first four games of the championship series. Then came Game Five, one of the most memorable games I have ever broadcast.

The 82-game season and the playoff grind had taken its toll on both teams. Key players were bothered by nagging injuries, the most significant being Reed's aching knee, a chronic problem that could not improve until the nightly battering he exposed it to finally ended. In the first period the Knicks fell behind by 10 points and, although that was bad, things quickly got worse.

With less than four minutes remaining in the first period, DeBusschere hit Reed with a pass, and the Knick center cut for the basket. But as he turned, he slipped and crumpled to the floor, his face framed in anguish. "And . . . Reed is hurt," I said into the microphone. "Play continues . . . but Reed is down."

Willis tried gamely to get up and rejoin the play, but his body wouldn't cooperate. He had pulled a muscle in his right hip, and the pain was spread all over his face. When play stopped, Trainer Danny Whelan and Coach Red Holzman rushed to Reed's side. Quickly, Dr. James Parkes was summoned, and he and Whelan led Reed off the court as the fans cheered their fallen hero. But the cheers were empty for without Reed the Knicks seemed doomed, and from the way Willis was walking, they certainly were going to be without him for a while.

Down 10 points with Reed, the Knicks could hardly expect to challenge the Lakers without their leader. Many teams would have folded their tents and surrendered, facing the impossible situation that Reed's injury had imposed. But those Knicks were made of a tough fiber. They were constructed by Holzman as a five-man team that won its games not because of the efforts of a single superstar but because of the unselfish, team-play concept that often drove less-disciplined teams slightly daffy. And, if ever that approach was tested, it was this night.

With Reed gone, the first job was to prevent the Lakers from turning the game into a rout. The Knicks, who would use five different players at center against Chamberlain before this memorable night was over, somehow managed that. Trailing by 10 points when Reed went out, they reached halftime down by 13. It was practically a moral victory considering that most people in the Garden had figured New York was out of it for the game and the series, when Reed limped off the court.

For the second half the Knicks went to a 1-3-1 attack, surrounding Chamberlain with shooters. The plan was to use Frazier at the top of the key, Bradley at the foul line, and DeBusschere in close. It was a strategy suggested by Bradley and designed to use to the utmost the weapons the Knicks still had left in their arsenal.

Facing the strange alignment more suited for a high school game than the fifth game of the NBA's championship round, the Lakers lost their poise. They made elementary mistakes, repeatedly turning the ball over to the Knicks. And New York cashed in on every break as the crowd roared its approval. Soon the 13-point bulge had been reduced to seven, and the fans were picking up the momentum, rattling the Lakers and encouraging the Knicks. They can only fit 19,000 fans in Madison Square Garden for basketball, but it sounded like the entire city of New York chanting, "Let's Go, Knicks!"

Los Angeles was still seven points ahead at the start of the fourth quarter and built the lead to nine. But the Knicks roared back, keeping the pressure on. The Lakers weren't the only ones feeling it. In the broadcast booth the cool, collected play-by-play man wasn't exactly the picture of nonchalance. I did my scheduled station break right on time, and routinely plugged WHN, our regular outlet, instead of WNBC, which was broadcasting this game. The result was a wakeup poke in the ribs from statistician Bob Meyer, who at least knew whose watts we were using at the time.

When the action resumed, so did the Los Angeles' turnovers. Point by point, New York whittled down the Laker lead and soon, it had completely evaporated. With eight minutes left the Knicks caught them at 87 on a basket by Bradley, and went ahead a few seconds later at 93-91, again thanks to the man his teammates called Dollar Bill. That was a reminder of the huge bonus the Knicks had paid Bradley. But on this tumultuous night, he was worth every penny.

By the time the clock was ticking off the game's final seconds, the Knicks had a seven-point lead and had sealed an improbable if not impossible victory. It was like New Year's Eve in May, with the fans spilling over the Garden floor chanting "We're Number One." The story of the game was told in a couple of vital statistics. There were 30 Los Angeles turnovers, 19 in the second half. Between them, West and Chamberlain had attempted only five shots in the second half. The Knicks' devastating defense had rescued them from a seemingly hopeless dilemma.

Back in Los Angeles for Game Six the Lakers regrouped and tied the seesaw series. The rotating corps of centers replacing Reed were burned for 45 points and 27 rebounds by Chamberlain. West threw in 33, and the Lakers won in a walk, 135-113. That sent the series down to one last game, a winner-take-all showdown in Madison Square Garden.

An army of medical personnel worked feverishly over Reed, trying to get enough mobility into his leg so he could at least dress for the seventh game. There were hot packs, massages, ultrasound treatments, every method modern medicine could come up with to cajole one more game out of that aching knee. Two hours before game-time, with the cavernous arena empty, he walked out on the court and tried a few easy shots. Then he returned to the dressing room for one more cortisone injection.

Before the game, the press room was buzzing with rumors. Reed would start. Reed would dress but not start. Reed couldn't play if his life, much less the NBA title, depended on it. Anything you wanted to hear was there to be heard. And it was the same thing in the Garden as it began filling up with fans. There was electricity in the air—the kind of excitement only a seventh game can create. And it was compounded by the Reed factor. Would he play? Could he play? Nobody knew, except Willis himself.

The Knicks and Lakers took the court for their pregame warmup, and Reed was conspicuous by his absence. Both teams worked out with the casual cool that basketball players always display, whether it's the first game of the season or the last one with the championship on the line. Some wore their sweat suits, some practiced layups, some stood at the foul line, tossing free throws. But all of them would look over ever so often to the runway leading to the dressing room, their eyes searching for the missing man, No. 19 in the Knicks' home, white uniform.

The digital clock at the end of the arena indicated 7:27, about three minutes before the introductions were to begin, when the crowd began to roar. The noise started in the upper reaches of the building, near our broadcast location, and spilled down section by section until it hit courtside. In an instant, the Garden was engulfed in noise as Reed, trotting ever so gingerly, appeared. Both teams stopped warming up—that's how dramatic the moment was. Reed grabbed a ball and flipped it casually into the basket as the building all but exploded.

When the game started, Reed was at center for the Knicks. He wasn't moving very well, but his presence on the court gave the team and the fans an emotional boost that was phenomenal. And a few moments later, he nearly brought down the building. Trailing a Knick break downcourt, Reed arrived at the foul line just in time to grab a pass from Dave DeBusschere. He jumped gently and popped a soft left-handed shot. It swished through the basket cleanly, and the Knicks were in front. The Garden was bedlam. Moments later the scene was repeated. Again, Reed connected, this time on a 20-foot jumper.

He did not score another point that night. He did not have to. He had done his job. He had given his team the emotional lift it needed. Playing on one leg with more courage than I have ever seen an athlete possess, Reed had ignited his team. He had scored four points on the scoreboard, but they had the effect of 400. By halftime, the Knicks had blown the Lakers right out of the building and were leading, 61-37. At the start of the second half, Reed again did not appear for the warmups and when the teams got set for the jump ball, Nate Bowman was at center for the Knicks. Then, with the same kind of dramatic flair he had displayed at the start of the game, Reed arrived. He took Bowman's spot for the tap as the Garden went absolutely bananas.

Willis played only six minutes in the second half and 27 for the night. But he was as much responsible for the 113-99 victory as any player on the club. And when the final seconds ticked off, the Knicks were world champions, and I had finished the most memorable play-by-play games of my career—the remarkable fifth-game comeback and the dramatic seventh-game clincher.

The Knicks repeated their championship in 1972-73, with basically the same team constructed around Reed, Frazier, DeBusschere, and Bradley. Barnett was near retirement and Frazier's new backcourt partner was Earl "The Pearl" Monroe, acquired in a trade with Baltimore. In another trade, Cazzie Russell was sent to Golden State in a deal that moved Jerry Lucas to New York. Lucas had been an All-American at Ohio State on the great team that included John Havlicek and Larry Siegfried. (One of the subs on that Buckeye team was Bobby Knight, who later became a big success as a college coach.)

Lucas is a personable, bright guy who seemed to be the perfect choice when NBC was looking for a color broadcaster to work with me in covering the 1975 NCAA Tournament. And he would have been, except for his alma mater. That's what got us in trouble.

In the quarterfinals, unbeaten Indiana, with a 31-game winning streak, was up against Kentucky, a tough, disciplined team that would be a severe test. We showed up a day before the game and routinely we decided to check out the clubs. That's a prerequisite for any broadcaster who hopes to do a decent job on a game. So, we headed for practice.

When we got to the Kentucky workout, Coach Joe B. Hall wouldn't let us in. The team simply would not practice while we were in the building, and when I asked Hall why, he pointed at Lucas. "Him, that's why," the coach said. What's wrong with Lucas, I wondered. The answer was: his alma mater and that little-used sub on the end of the Ohio State bench during Lucas' All-American days. Knight was now coaching Indiana, and Hall wasn't taking any chances with past school ties. He wasn't letting anybody from Indiana near his team, much less the old teammate of the Hoosier's coach.

Whatever Hall and Kentucky were working on in those secret practices must have been the right formula. In the quarterfinals, the Wildcats beat Indiana by two points, ending the nation's longest collegiate winning streak. Knight, never a picture of tranquility on the bench, stormed and stamped his way up and down the sidelines and in the stands, while his wife wept. It was a dramatic moment in college basketball history, and I was privileged to do the play-by-play.

Lucas spent three years in New York and then retired. DeBusschere quit to become commissioner of the American Basketball Association and was one of the key men in the merger of the two leagues. Reed's aches and pains forced him to quit in 1974, and he went on to become coach of the Knicks. Bradley left after 1976-77 season to enter politics. The last of the Old Guard was Frazier, the backcourt magician nicknamed Clyde by New York's basketball cognoscenti, who marveled at his stylish dress and cool play.

Frazier had been a direct product of the Garden's sponsorship of the National Invitation Tournament. He had arrived at the NIT with Southern Illinois in 1967 and sparked the small midwestern school to the tournament title in the last NIT played in the old Madison Square Garden. He was named the Most Valuable Player, and not long afterwards the Knicks made him their No. 1 choice in the NBA draft.

Frazier and the Knicks' crowds were made for each other. He was the pulsebeat of the Knicks, and the fans knew it. The club looked to Clyde for leadership, and he provided it with the poise of a guard who had been playing in the NBA forever. There is no question that New Yorks' two championships were molded around the backcourt play of Frazier, a cool customer under even the most difficult circumstances.

His teammates hung the Clyde nickname on Frazier, comparing his cool, stylish dress with Warren Beatty's film portrait of the gangster Clyde Barrow in the movie *Bonnie and Clyde*. And, like Barrow, Frazier, too, was a thief—of errant passes and loose basketballs.

As the others dropped off, one by one, it became inevitable that Frazier, too, one day would be leaving the Garden and the Knicks. He suffered through a couple of difficult seasons, giving up captaincy of the team at one point and undergoing considerable criticism from fans and the press when the easy style he always displayed had seemed to drift into boredom. The end finally came just before the start of the 1977-78 season when Clyde was sent to Cleveland as compensation for the Knicks signing free agent Jim Cleamons. It had the effect of a simple one-for-one trade, although the semantics have changed in today's world of free agency.

By the luck of the NBA schedule, 10 days after he was dealt to Cleveland, Frazier returned to the Garden with the Cavaliers to play against the Knicks. I scheduled an interview with Clyde before the game for television, and he was clearly nervous, an unusual situation for a guy so identified with being cool. He said he didn't know how the fans would react to him. He knew he had gone through a couple of bad years and wasn't sure whether the fans would remember *that* Clyde or the one who captivated them on two championship Knick teams. I told him not to be concerned, that they'd go crazy for him. And they did exactly that when announcer John Condon introduced him at the start of the game. Clyde, with his sense of, and flair for, the dramatic, reacted perfectly to the excitement, leading Cleveland to an overtime victory over the Knicks with a spectacular 28-point game.

Frazier's return was remarkable, but nothing like the night goalie Eddie Giacomin came back to the Garden to play against the New York Rangers. Giacomin had been the backbone of the Rangers for a decade, the man around whom the organization built a Stanley Cup contender. He had come to the team as a journeyman minor leaguer and nearly got booed right back to the bushes in his first year. But eventually Giacomin settled down to become one of the very best netminders. He led the Rangers into nine consecutive playoffs, shared the Vezina Trophy in 1971, and was virtually a cornerstone of the franchise. Balcony fans at the Garden delighted in saluting his goaltending acrobatics with chants of "Ed-die, Ed-die, Ed-die," a cheer patterned after the Knick fans' "Dee-fense, Dee-fense, Dee-fense."

The Ranger teams of the later 1960s and early 1970s were powerhouses, but unfortunately they always came up short in the playoffs. And eventually, age began creeping up on them, and old standbys like Vic Hadfield, Rod Seiling, Jim Neilson, and others were traded away. Giacomin's turn came on Friday, October 31, 1975—Halloween night. He was sent to Detroit on waivers, and two nights later, in the Garden to play the Rangers were the Red Wings with their new goalie.

Giacomin spent Saturday trying to decide whether to report to the Red Wings or to call it a career. He was, after all, 36 years old and had little more to prove in the NHL. But friends and family convinced him to stick with it, and two days later he skated onto the Garden ice wearing the unfamiliar flame-red sweater of the Red Wings, ready to face the team he had played for so memorably barely 48 hours earlier.

Anyone who was in the Garden that night will never forget it. The return of Walt Frazier was different. The rumors of his departure had been all over town for quite some time, and it was just a matter of where and when he would go. Giacomin's waiver sale, on the other hand, was a shocker. The fans had 10 days to digest the Frazier deal. Giacomin was back in the building only two days after he was sold, and the emotion of that night was unbelievable.

I expected the fans to cheer Eddie. But the response they gave him was beyond simple cheering. It bordered on hysteria. The crowd was like a lynch mob, rooting madly for Giacomin and Detroit and booing everything the Rangers did. It was as if the Red Wings and not the Rangers were the home team that night. The emotion of the moment was enormous, and it simply overcame Giacomin. As he stood, listening to the chant of "Ed-die, Ed-die, Ed-die," drowning out the strains of the national anthem, tears streamed down his face.

"I've never been an emotional man, but I couldn't hold back," Giacomin told reporters after the game. And I'm sure his weren't the only tears that flowed in the Garden that night. Giacomin, playing on the adrenalin of the situation, blocked 42 shots and backstopped the Red Wings to a 6-4 victory. "This is a day I'll never forget as long as I live," he said.

And the play-by-play man felt the same way. Eddie asked me for a play-by-play cassette of the game, and I guess he's still listening to it.

Probably the most difficult broadcasting assignment is hockey overtime. The game ends in a flash. In football, a team often drives toward the winning TD the way Baltimore did against the New York Giants in that famous 1958 playoff. In basketball, a team often builds a lead to gain its overtime victory. But in hockey, one shot and it's all over . . . just like that. Occasionally, though, you can feel that goal coming. That was the way it happened in the fourth game of the 1977 Stanley Cup championship series between the Boston Bruins and Montreal Canadiens.

The Canadiens had won the first three games of the series and only an outstanding performance by the Bruins had forced Game Four into overtime. Now the Canadiens needed one more goal to wrap up another Cup, and they were going after it aggressively. The puck was in Boston's zone and the Canadiens were doing what they do best—swarming around like a fleet of dive bombers, zipping after the puck and beating the Bruins to the punch.

Boston goalie Gerry Cheevers looked like a frontiersman standing in front of his cabin, trying to fight off an Indian raid. Tim Ryan and I, broadcasting the game on the National Hockey League network, exchanged glances and nodded. We could both see what was coming. Ryan was doing the play-by-play, when Guy Lafleur and Steve Shutt rushed into the corner and swept the puck back to Jacques Lemaire, left unguarded at the right side. Lemaire's shot was strong and true, and Ryan captured hockey's most exciting moment, crying into his microphone, "Lemaire shoots . . . He scores . . . and the Canadiens win the Stanley Cup!"

That's the ultimate. What can possibly top that for a player or, for that matter, a broadcaster? It is the final moment when the sport's championship rests on a single shot. It was sudden death for the Bruins and a slice of hockey history for Lemaire, who'll never forget the moment he won the Stanley Cup for the Canadiens. And the moment will be every bit as memorable for Ryan. I know because I've broadcast my share of overtime games. During the 1977 playoffs alone I had three OT games—the final one when Lemaire clinched the Cup for Montreal, the semifinal opener when Rick Middleton beat

Philadelphia for Boston, and a quarterfinal game in which Toronto's Lanny McDonald beat the Flyers.

Ryan had a unique situation in that final game when the Canadiens finished off the Bruins. He actually had a chance to prepare for the ending. It was almost telegraphed. The Bruins were running around in their own end kind of helter-skelter, and the way the Canadiens were driving, you could just feel the goal coming. It was a question of which Montreal player would score it and just how soon it would happen. I remember one overtime game, though, in which I had almost no time to prepare for the finish. That was because it would be the fastest overtime in NHL history.

That happened in 1974 when the New York Islanders were playing my team, the New York Rangers, in the opening round of the playoffs. That first round is two out of three, and NHL people like to call it Russian roulette. This is the ultimate short series and it is played like sudden-death hockey almost from the opening faceoff. One mistake can be fatal and, in a short series, you just can't afford the luxury of making them.

The Islanders were in their third year of operation in 1974 and still trying to overcome the memories of their disastrous first season when they had managed only twelve victories—the poorest record in NHL history. The Rangers were their big-city brethren, successful and smug. The first-round matchup was a natural, and it turned out to be one of the most memorable series in Stanley Cup history.

The Islanders stunned the Rangers in the opening game, beating them in their own building, Madison Square Garden. But Game Two went to the Rangers in the Nassau Coliseum. So, it all came down to the Russian roulette showdown—Game Three in the Garden.

The hustling young Islanders came out for the kill and built a 3-0 lead after two periods. But the veteran Rangers weren't going to die easily. They marshaled their efforts into 20 superb minutes of hockey in which they scored three goals to tie the game and send it into overtime. This was truly sudden death because the overtime loser would be done for the season. But there was more involved. The veteran Rangers were hanging on for one last hurrah. The ambitious Islanders were on the threshold of becoming legitimate Cup contenders.

I think everybody in Madison Square Garden that night was aware of the mini-morality play we were witnessing. This was like two ships passing in the night. There was more than a hockey game at stake here. Much more.

Often I'll leave the broadcast booth between periods of a game to get a breather. But I decided to stay put this time as the Rangers and Islanders headed for their dressing rooms after that third period. I didn't want to get caught in a crowd trying to get back to the booth. I wanted to be ready as soon as they dropped that puck, and it's a good thing I was.

In the overtime, the Rangers were skating from my right to my left and Eddie Giacomin was defending the goal at the Eighth Avenue end of Madison Square Garden. People were still making their way down the aisles and back to their seats when the puck was dropped. It skittered into the Rangers' end and—just my luck—wound up in the near corner of the rink where my view was obscured by the milling fans.

" . . . Off the face, it's shot in into the Ranger end . . . " I began the play-by-play routinely. But then, when it went into the corner, I lost the puck for a moment and I remember standing up, trying to locate it. The Rangers were doing the same thing.

" . . . Vickers passes the puck . . . " Suddenly Parise swooped on it. My voice reacted. "Intercepted by Parise . . . in front of the net . . . Parise shoots . . . he scores!"

In 11 seconds, it was over. There was no time to be prepared. The end came as a total shock to the fans, the Rangers, and to me. It was bang-bang—the fastest overtime goal in Stanley Cup history. I got excited because I had an obligation to do that for the Islanders and for their fans. The crowd, of course, was almost silent. Everybody had expected the Rangers to win, especially after that third-period comeback. Certainly the Rangers never anticipated anything else, and I remember watching them bang their sticks on the ice while the Islanders swarmed over the boards, mobbing J. P. Parise, who scored the winning goal.

That was a symbolic moment for both teams and for hockey in New York. Suddenly, the Islanders were the haves and the Rangers were the have-nots. I sensed the transition and tried to transmit it to the listeners. The Rangers had to make changes, and it was obvious that until they could be rebuilt, hockey excitement in New York would belong to the hustling, young Islanders who had won with the fastest overtime goal.

Five years later, in 1979, the Rangers and Islanders met in another Stanley Cup series that completely captured New York. This time it was the playoff semifinals instead of the 2-out-of-3 preliminary round, and the tables were turned. Now the Rangers, rebuilt by a new management team headed by Fred Shero, were the longshot underdogs, and the Islanders, who had the best record in the NHL during the 1978-79 season, were the favorites.

The Islanders were led by center Bryan Trottier, the NHL scoring champion, Mike Bossy, the league's top goal-scorer, and Denis Potvin, the NHL's best defenseman. Stopping them would be a tall order but the Rangers, fresh off a strong series against Los Angeles and Philadelphia, were confident. They had a hot goaltender in big John Davidson, and sometimes, that's all it takes.

Davidson had been the difference in a two-game sweep of the Kings, and the same thing was true against the Flyers when the Rangers won four straight after dropping the overtime opener. And almost before they knew it, the surprising Rangers were in the final four, matched against their suburban neighbors, the Islanders. Some called it the Long Island Railroad series and it put hockey on the front pages in New York. The survivor would play for hockey's most cherished trophy, the Stanley Cup.

The Rangers, playing on momentum, stunned the Islanders by winning the opener on Long Island. Only an overtime goal by Potvin prevented the Rangers from taking a 2-0 lead home to Madison Square Garden. But all they wanted was a split in the Nassau Coliseum and they had that. Game Three went to New York but again the Islanders tied the series when they won the fourth contest in overtime on a goal by Bobby Nystrom. The pivotal fifth game was played on Long Island but again the Rangers prevailed, with a late goal by Anders Hedberg proving the difference.

I don't think I will ever forget the roar of the crowd in Madison Square Garden the night of the sixth game when the Rangers finished the Islanders off and advanced to the finals. The noise was deafening as New York's hockey fans saluted what seemed a team of destiny. For the first time since 1972, the Rangers would play for the Stanley Cup.

In the finals, the Rangers played Montreal and the momentum continued when they beat the Canadiens in their own building in Game One. In Game Two, the Rangers jumped to a 2-0 lead and for the first time I felt they could really win the Cup. I couldn't believe what was happening. It was astounding. But suddenly, it all turned around. Before the end of the first period, the Canadiens had struck back for three goals to take a 3-2 lead. It was all downhill after that. The bubble burst in a hurry. Montreal won that game and the next three and, all too quickly, The Little Miracle of 33rd Street was over.

That unlikely Ranger run at the Cup in 1979 was, over a long stretch, the most enjoyable broadcast experience I've had since the 1969-70 Knicks won the NBA championship. You develop a feeling for a team, and the Rangers were a really good group of guys. Davidson, captain Dave Maloney, and veteran Phil Esposito became the town's best-known athletes. Fred Shero was a mysterious genius whose answers to questions often captured the essence of the situation. During the Islander series, high-scorer Mike Bossy was completely shackled by the Rangers. Shero was asked about Bossy's dilemma. He smiled benignly and replied: "That's not my problem."

Even though they had lost the Cup to the Canadiens, the Rangers recaptured New York by knocking off the Islanders. It was the ultimate payback for J. P. Parise's goal which had sent the Rangers reeling out of the playoffs the last time these two teams played.

That particular sudden-death goal left a bitter taste in the mouths of the Rangers and their fans. But there was another overtime I can remember that ended much more pleasantly for Madison Square Garden's hockey club. That was in 1971, when the Rangers played the Chicago Black Hawks in the semifinal series. Montreal kayoed the defending champion Boston Bruins in the first round, so we knew there was going to be a new Cup winner. The Rangers felt it might as well be them.

But the Black Hawks were no pushovers in those days. Bobby Hull was still with them, and Stan Mikita, a craftsman at center ice, was at the top of his game. The defense had a Mutt 'n Jeff combination of short Pat Stapleton and tall Bill White that was just about the best in the league.

The Rangers were learning firsthand just how good Chicago was. After Pete Stemkowski's overtime goal had won the first game of the series, the Hawks took three of the next four. So in Game Six, New York faced elimination. When a Stanley Cup series gets down to the short strokes like that, you can expect cautious play by both clubs. But I don't think anybody in the building could have expected what the Rangers and Black Hawks were about to supply.

Tied after three periods, the teams steamed into overtime. Goalies Tony Esposito for Chicago and Eddie Giacomin for New York were brilliant in the first extra period. The checking was tight and the two teams played tough, basic hockey, check-for-check. The Rangers' best chances belonged to their big line—Jean Ratelle, Rod Gilbert, and Vic Hadfield. But Esposito refused to be budged. The Hull brothers, Bobby and Dennis, both had good opportunities but couldn't connect on Giacomin.

In the second overtime, it was more of the same. Tough, fundamental hockey, good saves and, most important, no goals. Midway through the period, Mikita had a wide open net since Giacomin was kayoed from a shot that cracked him in the mask. Incredibly, Mikita's shot banged off one post, glanced across the empty goal mouth, and ricocheted harmlessly off the other. Mikita smashed his stick over the crossbar, shattering it in anger over the remarkable sequence.

With the Garden clock ticking its way toward midnight, I remember doing something on the broadcast that was extremely unusual for me. I turned personal. My wife Benita and I had left our son in the care of a young baby sitter. We weren't concerned about him, but I do recall saying over the air, "Mike, we're gonna be a little late tonight."

The third overtime started slowly. The game had begun at 7:35 so the teams had been battling for more than four hours, and I guess everybody was getting a little groggy. Giacomin made an early save, and it was to be the last one he would make that night.

The puck skittered up ice and a tough, low shot brought Esposito out to the right corner of his net for the save. He kicked the puck away neatly but it rebounded right to Stemkowski, who was cutting for the net. Esposito tried desperately to react, but Stemkowski's stick was too quick. Always one of the game's top playoff performers, Stemmer had nudged the winning goal into the Black Hawk net. The longest game in modern Ranger history was over and the building went slightly bananas.

The roar was deafening, and I'm not entirely sure I could be heard above it. I know I was shouting into the microphone, trying to overcome the din. " . . . Peter Stemkowski's rebound goal at 1:29 of the third overtime wins it for the Rangers . . . " I remember pronouncing Stemmer's name slowly, breaking it into syllables to add to the drama.

When the mob scene on the ice and in the stands had cleared and a semblance of sanity returned to the Garden, I was still on the air with my color man, Hall of Fame referee Bill Chadwick, who was nicknamed The Big Whistle. We tried to analyze the significance of the win coming so dramatically and what effect it would have on the Rangers in Game Seven. We both agreed that the emotional nature of the victory, coming the way it did in triple overtime, would give New York a tremendous edge in momentum for that final game. I remember both of us saying that there was no way the club could be beaten after that game.

A lot we knew. The Rangers went to Chicago for Game Seven and, despite the Albert-Chadwick can't-miss prediction, New York dropped a 4-2 decision and the playoff series.

That memorable series occurred during one of the most successful stretches in Ranger history—the 1967-75 era, when the team reached the playoffs for nine consecutive seasons. I was fortunate enough to be the radio voice of the club throughout that era of success, and one of the early magic moments had come in that very first playoff year—1967.

New York played Montreal in the first round of the playoffs that year, and the powerful Canadiens won the first three games of the series. Game Four was tied at the end of regulation time and so the two teams headed into an extra period—my first taste of sudden-death broadcasting.

I have two vivid memories of that extra period. The first one occurred when Red Berenson, who had not scored a goal all season for the Rangers, broke in on Montreal goalie Rogatien Vachon. Berenson made a textbook move and had Vachon at his mercy. My voice rose in anticipation as Berenson pulled the trigger. But luck was on Vachon's side. The puck plunked harmlessly off the post and play continued—but not for long. The Canadiens must have been ignited by Berenson's near miss. They came roaring down the ice and quickly scored the clinching goal. The man who put the final nail in New York's coffin that season was John Ferguson—the same Ferguson who was put in charge of the team's reconstruction in 1976. It's funny how fate works sometimes. Funny, and memorable.

With no further introduction: Don Meredith, Howard Cosell, and Frank Gifford. (ABC)

# 10 COLOR MEN

One of the first things a newspaperman is taught is the difference in format between a morning paper's style and that of an evening paper. The morning paper is a straightforward account of the facts with few flourishes added, apart from columns. Its radio-television counterpart is the play-by-play man, whose job is strictly reportorial in nature, interspersed with a degree of personality and individual style. The afternoon paper, with a more leisurely deadline, meaning less pressure, has the time to weave interpretive insights into its stories. And its broadcast counterpart is the color man, whose job is to explain what happened, how it happened, and why it happened. The task is not an easy one.

Compared to the job of the color man, a play-by-play announcer's work is a cinch. All I have to do is follow the action—the football, or the basketball, or the puck—and tell the listener its progress from player to player and the outcome of each maneuver—goal, touchdown, basket, or whatever. I am a reporter. My color man is the analyst, the commentator whose explanation can complete the play-by-play picture for the listener. He has a vital job and the success or failure of a broadcast often rests squarely on his shoulders.

I have always felt that a color man should be a well-known personality who can qualify as an expert because of his credentials as a former athlete. Those credentials should establish his credibility. What qualifies him to be analyzing the action, unless he's been through it firsthand?

If I were a producer, selecting a candidate to be a color announcer, I'd have several qualities I'd look for, regardless of what sport he was going to be doing. My color man would have to be articulate, of course. That's basic. If he couldn't communicate with his audience, he could have the finest credentials in the world, but they wouldn't mean a thing. They'd melt like a cake of ice in July if he couldn't be understood by his listeners. Next, my man would have to have a sense of humor. He'd have to be loose and possess human qualities. Listeners don't appreciate listening to a lecture. Next, I'd want my color man to be objective—not a cheerleader.

I've been fortunate in hockey and basketball to work with two men who fit these qualifications perfectly. Hockey color man Sal Messina could work in a club's front office. He knows that much about the game. He knows the game as a player from his days as a goaltender, and he knows it from a technical standpoint because of his experience as a minor official. In basketball, my partner is Richie Guerin, one of the top players in the history of the New York Knicks and a former coach and general manager. Like Messina, he brings a depth of knowledge to his assignment, and it is a joy to work with pros like these two.

Some athletes and former athletes are as good as any professional announcer, especially at color-man duties. Those who come to mind immediately are Len Dawson, who worked with me on several NFL broadcasts; Don Drysdale, third man in the booth on ABC's Monday night baseball series; Joe Garagiola and Bob Uecker, a couple of mediocre catchers who rode their ordinary baseball careers into broadcasting stardom, and Rick Barry, who promises to be every bit as good behind the microphone as he is on the basketball court.

Don Meredith is ABC's football counterpart to Drysdale—the third man in the booth. Yet their roles on the broadcasts differ. Drysdale offers expertise. Meredith occupies a comedy role with Frank Gifford and Howard Cosell, and plays off them, particularly Cosell, for his appeal. Garagiola and Uecker are storytellers, and I think that is a particularly effective technique for a broadcaster. Those stories take the listeners behind the scenes, where they ordinarily cannot go.

Garagiola and Uecker also prove that a color broadcaster need not have been a star to be effective over the airwaves. But you do have to know what you're talking about. If you don't, you're in trouble. Your credibility will be shattered in no time and once that's gone, you become useless. But a knowledgeable color man can add a great deal to the show. In college

We're wired in for the College Basketball Game of the Week. My partner is color man Bucky Waters. (CHRIS SHERIDAN)

basketball, some of the best color men include Billy Packer, Bucky Waters, and John Andariese, none of whom is exactly a household name but each has vast knowledge of the sport.

Packer played college ball at Wake Forest; Waters coached at Duke and West Virginia; and Andariese played at Fordham. None were well-known nationally because they were not involved in professional basketball and their schools weren't exactly collegiate powerhouses that would attract nationwide attention. They established themselves because, quite simply, they are so good at what they do. Packer, Waters, and Andariese are honest analytical reporters who don't just point out the obvious. That's very important for a color man to remember. He's not there in the broadcast booth to explain the simple plays. The listener can probably do that for himself. The color man's task is to simplify the technical, intricate plays—to explain them in layman's language.

In football, the two trailblazers for color reporting were Al DeRogatis on radio and the late Paul Christman on television. DeRogatis was an offensive lineman during his playing days—one of those anonymous up-front guys who worked in pro football's trenches and knew the game inside out. Christman was a glamour halfback who brought a different perspective to the game. Each in his own way had an effect on a new profession. DeRo delighted in the technical aspects of pro football, the blackboard X's and O's that coaches diagram. Listening to him was like peeking in a playbook. Christman was more straightforward in his approach to the game and, I think, easier for the listeners to understand. Especially since they didn't have a playbook to refer to.

It's interesting that football color men are often players who performed a level or two below superstardom during their active careers. In New York, for example, offensive lineman Dave Herman and Sam DeLuca (in the preseason) are the radio and television color analysts for the Jets. The Giants use defensive back Dick Lynch on radio and running back Tucker Frederickson on preseason television. For a long time my radio partner with the Giants was Sam Huff, the onetime star linebacker, who delighted in breaking down the defensive plays, much the way he broke down offensive plays when he was playing.

Herman was one of the blockers who protected the delicate knees of quarterback Joe Namath, the colorful character who engineered one of pro football's most startling upsets—the 1969 Jets' Super Bowl victory over the Baltimore Colts. Namath, of course, is retired now and has dabbled in some broadcasting, although he's stayed away from covering football games. He would be great in that assignment because he has the stage presence required for the job. That is one of the important qualities a broadcaster must possess. An athlete who has that can step right behind a microphone.

Color broadcasters are used in both radio and television, and there is a distinct contrast in their duties in those two mediums. Radio is strictly audio, so the color man must be able to describe in words just what has happened. Like the play-by-play man, he must paint a word-picture and that is often difficult. On television, the color man works with replays, explaining the action that appears on the screen. He has a picture to work with, a picture that can show his listeners precisely what he's explaining. That makes the television color man's job easier in some ways yet more difficult in others. He has the picture to work with, which simplifies his task, but he must often describe intricate plays that the viewer can see before him and expects to have explained. That can be tough.

Basketball and football replays lend themselves best to color analysis. In baseball, the replays rarely point out any secrets because the nature of the game makes original action so wide open. But the color man's duty remains to point out details. On a steal, for example, it might be the placement of the tag or the position of the runner's slide. There's always something to say, something that will aid the viewer's understanding of just what has taken place. Besides analysis of individual plays, color men also have interview responsibilities. Ex-athletes all have had experience at being the subject in interviews—the interviewee. But that doesn't mean they will be good interviewers. This is a new role they're stepping into, a new profession. Sometimes, the reverse just doesn't work.

I remember Bill "Butch" van Breda Kolff, one of basketball's most animated coaches, in a brief stint as a color man. After a televised game, Bill had to go on the court for an interview, and fans began crowding around him as they often do following college games. Soon they were interfering with van Breda Kolff's interview, a fact that didn't exactly thrill the ex-coach. You could see him barely controlling a trigger temper that was so familiar to basketball referees with whom he'd had his share of disagreements. It took enormous poise for him to get out of there without having a fist fight.

Perhaps the most important part of a color man's job is his ability to establish rapport with the play-by-play announcer. There is a chemistry that is created between the two and that is so important to the success of their presentation. They must play off each other with a timing that is precise without being obvious. When they come across comfortably, without gaps and hesitation, then the broadcast team is doing the job the way it should be done. That smoothness comes from working over and over with the same partner. During the hockey and basketball season, I work with the same color men on radio for perhaps 50 or 60 broadcasts. You get to know your partner so well that the broadcast is almost scripted. I will deliberately say something that I know will lead the color man to logically carry it on to another point. You want to give him some place to go. You must leave him with something to say.

The play-by-play man and his color partner use hand signals to communicate with each other in the booth. Sometimes the play-by-play broadcaster will nod to his partner when he's about to lead him into the commentary. Or the color man might motion to indicate he has a thought to add, which cues the play-by-play man to weave him into the broadcast. Every so often, you step on each other's lines. That's inevitable when you're weaving the other guy in and out of the show. You obviously just try to keep that to a minimum.

That's one of the reasons I don't like the format of three men in a broadcast booth. Too often, a third man feels he must justify his presence and will talk when really what he has to say is superfluous. Also, if the third man doesn't have a distinctive voice it can lead to aural confusion. And why do you need two analyses? I think it's just too much. It becomes broadcast overkill, and the victim can be the show.

One of the most difficult jobs for the color man is to fit comfortably in the presentation. In the somewhat spartan situations you work with on local radio, when the play-by-play man, his color partner, the statistician and the engineer may be the only men in the broadcast booth, it becomes a challenging job of orchestration for the two announcers. You pick your spots, and you must be careful to avoid situations in which you might miss part of the action while the color commentator is talking. Sometimes you miss. If that happens, you might be an instant off on the play-by-play and so you play catch-up, using the shortest words to close the gap as quickly as possible. It's a knack that you can only pick up through experience.

On television, the producer is hooked into your earphone, and he will suggest ways to involve the color man. He might suggest an idea the color man could interject at a particular moment in the action. Or he might instruct the play-by-play man to involve his partner by asking a specific question. On TV, you want the color expert talking over the replays, explaining the action. Again, it's a matter of orchestration. This is, remember, a show that you want to be smooth and entertaining as well as informative.

The best way to introduce the color man is right at the start of the broadcast. That way, you immediately establish his presence as part of the broadcast team. A favorite technique of many play-by-play announcers to bring the color man into the picture is to let him handle the starting lineups. That is a comfortable, easy way to introduce him to the audience and lead into the start of the game.

Perhaps the most important quality for a color man to possess is the ability to remain pertinent. Too many of them say something simply because they feel an obligation to say something. That's when silence would be golden. It is better to say nothing at all if you have nothing at all to say.

One of the advantages that ex-athletes have as color men is their ability to be anecdotal on the air. They can tell stories and they enjoy that role, which is particularly effective during a baseball game when rain causes a delay in play.

There is no formula that guarantees success for retired athletes behind a microphone. Some succeed and some don't, and athletic ability has absolutely nothing to do with it. Just ask Garagiola and Uecker. Perhaps the best examples of the two ends of the spectrum for retired athletes who try broadcasting after their active careers are Tony Kubek and Sandy Koufax.

Kubek was a better-than-average infielder during the New York Yankee glory years, and is now an outstanding baseball announcer. Koufax was a Hall of Fame pitcher with the Los Angeles Dodgers, who washed out when he tried announcing. I guess it has something to do with personalities. Kubek is an outgoing, friendly guy who'll talk baseball with anybody at any time. That's perfect for the broadcasting role he occupies. Koufax is a private, almost shy man, who let his pitching do his talking. That was fine when he was playing but just didn't work when he tried television color announcing.

Kubek's sincere, candid approach got him into hot water with the New York Yankees' front office in spring training before the 1978 baseball season. It was a silly matter, really, and a case of overreaction on the part of Yankee owner George Steinbrenner. Kubek, who diligently tours training camps to give himself background on the teams, was interviewed by a local reporter at the Yankees' Fort Lauderdale, Florida camp, and said some things that were critical of Steinbrenner. The Yankee owner saw the story and immediately ordered his players not to grant interviews to Kubek. I can understand Steinbrenner being angry, but his reaction was out of proportion.

When a color man is shut off from player interviews he is in trouble. Kubek, to his credit, did not take Steinbrenner's gag lying down. He spoke out against it and that created pressure that forced the Yankee front office to beat a strategic retreat from a rather touchy position.

What the ball club forgot was that Kubek is an individual who works for a network, not a team. It's not his job to protect any

Curt Gowdy (left) and Tony Kubek in their heyday as play-by-play and color man, respectively, for Major League Baseball's Game of the Week. (NBC)

teams or front office people, and he is entitled to express his opinions on any subject he chooses, Steinbrenner and the Yankees notwithstanding. That can often be one of the problems with broadcasting baseball for one club. Some teams expect you to be a cheerleader and a salesman. They don't realize fans see right through this. They make it impossible to maintain the objective stance I think a reporter—whether on radio and television or one who communicates in print—should maintain. All the owners are interested in is filling up those empty seats, you are their pipeline to the public and that should be your job. In the sports I've done, I don't face that pressure. I'd have difficulty with that if I did. Kubek, who doesn't work for the Yankees, felt no need to be anything but frank when a reporter asked his opinion of the club's management. There's nothing wrong with that, unless you're management and are sensitive.

Kubek's comments offered the kind of in-depth analysis a color broadcaster is supposed to provide. The only difference was that they appeared in print instead of going over the airwaves. But team managements have been criticized forever by newspapermen whose papers don't pay a dime for the right to cover and report on games. Television and radio pays millions of dollars for those rights. Why shouldn't that media's reporters have the same commentary rights? And if the commentary is going to be on the Yankees, who would be better qualified to make it than Kubek, who spent his entire major league career playing for that team?

In my career, which has included stints as a disc jockey and straight news reader, I've occasionally done color as well. But really, I'd rule myself out of that role. I can be a reporter, but I can't be an expert. I'm just not qualified for that. The color man should be an expert. That's the reason he's there in the first place, to dress up my play-by-play with analysis. That's his job and he can do it better than I.

# 11 DEAR MARV

"**I** watched your interview with Jimmy Connors and I was very disappointed in you. I didn't think you would stoop to 'yellow journalism.'"

"It was refreshing to see you honestly, and without malice, inform Jimmy Connors of what New York City's opinion of him is. There is no longer any doubt that anyone unfamiliar with the antics of Connors learned quickly how immature he really is."

"Your interview with Connors was not sports, but more like Rona Barrett."

"Congratulations. You were the first to put hard questions to Connors and not let him edit the questioning."

Letters . . . we get letters . . . we get lots and lots of letters. That was the theme song for a segment of the old *Perry Como Show* on TV, but it could apply to most people in radio and television, and that includes sportscasters. I get literally thousands of letters each year, some of them from people who listen to my play-by-play broadcasts on radio and TV and some of them from folks who watch my sports segments on evening news shows. I get reaction to almost anything I do or say and usually that reaction varies, as in the case of Jimmy Connors. When that happens, I know I'm doing my job properly, because you can't please everybody if you're an honest, straightforward reporter. Somebody is always going to have a complaint.

Sometimes listeners complain if I criticize their favorite team or player. They take it as a personal affront if I suggest on the air that a particular play was something short of textbook technique. But there's nothing I can do about it. My training is to report what happened, and I can't change it to suit the listeners. Some hometown, rah-rah broadcasters might, but that's not my style.

Once, after working an NCAA basketball playoff between Kentucky and Indiana, I got a batch of letters. Some people thought I was too pro-Indiana in that broadcast. Others insisted that I was flagrantly in Kentucky's corner. That convinced me that I had done the game just the way I wanted to—right down the middle.

For years, New York's only pro basketball team was the Knicks, and the only pro hockey club was the Rangers. Those are the two Madison Square Garden teams for whom I do play-by-play broadcasts during the winter season. As major league sports expanded, the New York area picked up two new franchises, the Islanders in the National Hockey League, and the Nets, who first played in the old American Basketball Association and then were added to the National Basketball Association when the ABA went out of business.

Now, the proximity of Madison Square Garden to the NBC broadcast studios makes it a simple matter to bring in Knicks and Rangers players for postgame interviews. The Islanders play on Long Island and the Nets in New Jersey, neither exactly an accessible site for importing athletes in time for the late newscasts. What's more, the Nets' move to New Jersey did not include frequent cable television coverage that would provide the feeds for highlights. Yet we constantly get complaints that we are ignoring the two new teams and favoring the Knicks and Rangers, both of whom are covered for every home game on cable, which can supply taped highlights. Sometimes we send our own film crews. You can't very well show highlights of a team that doesn't have games televised.

I make it a practice to answer all of my mail, although, because of the volume, it sometimes takes time to get around to all of it. My wife, Benita, helps a lot in the letter-writing department. I feel it's important to answer the mail. If people take the time to write, then I have to find the time to answer them. And the customers always write. Here are some examples:

Dear Mr. Albert,

We have admired your work as a sportscaster and play-by-play announcer for some time and we would like to include some of your work in a project we have undertaken.

We are assembling a time capsule which will contain various materials typical of the era in which we live. We would like to have you represented in this capsule. Would it be possible to secure a tape of your work for inclusion?

> Sincerely,
> RN Foundation
> Philadelphia, Pennsylvania

I guess there is only so much you can do to make yourself look pretty. (RICHARD PILLING)

Dear Marv,

When I saw you on the 6 o'clock news tonight, I decided that I *had* to write to you. I have wanted to write many times before but my husband, who thinks I'm crazy, always talked me out of it. But tonight was the last straw. *Your hair looks terrible!*

When you got in front of the camera the hairspray you used was *glistening!*

Marv, I'm not trying to insult you. I love you truly, so please, for your own sake, find another hairdresser.

Love,
RI
New York, New York

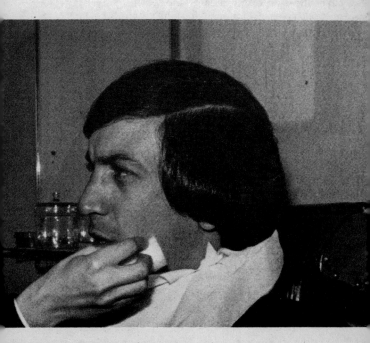

Dear Marv Albert,

Is your cameraman mad with you? He has had you badly out of focus on the 11 p.m. news for the past week. This shouldn't happen to a nice boy like you.

> Sincerely,
> BT
> New York, New York

---

Dear Marv,

Until a few months ago I had no idea who you were. That's because as soon as the sports report came on, off went the TV. You see, I have a slight problem, and that happens to be that I detest sports. I'm sure it's all psychological, but I won't go into that. Almost a year ago, I met the man of my dreams and we have a blissful relationship except for one thing—he's a sports fanatic!! Every night it's the same thing—the *Post* and Marv Albert. After several months of exposure to your sports report, I have to admit, I still hate sports but I love you. When we go to games at the Garden, I always look for you, and when there's a game on TV, we tune out the TV announcer and listen to you on the radio. I've picked up a lot of useful information from listening and I actually find myself looking forward to seeing you every night.

To get back to my problem, I was wondering if you could help me. Could you possibly recommend some kind of instructional books on football, hockey (the only sport I really enjoy), and basketball. If you can't help me there, I know a super Japanese restaurant on 55th Street. If you're ever free for lunch, and in the mood for Japanese food, it would be a real thrill for me to meet you. I hope that doesn't sound too aggressive, but I'm very serious about learning and developing an interest in sports, and if I can't learn from a book, what better way than to learn from you.

> Sincerely,
> SM
> New York, New York

Dear Marv Alpert (sic)

I just had to write you after the Islanders game Saturday night to tell you that your predictions are the same as the Kiss of Death. In the future, please predict non-New York teams as the winner. You may not be right but at least we'll have a better chance of winning.

Sincerely,
FP
Staten Island, New York

––––––––

Dear Marv,

When a pitcher gets knocked around in a few games I fail to hear the media—and mostly I am interested in you—say he is "flat," or "asleep," or "disinterested," or "complacent," or "unmotivated," or "lethargic," or "not working hard enough," or "ruined by a long term, fat contract," or "not wanting to win as much as the opposition," among others. Why, why, why, why are these terms only applicable to hockey, especially the Islanders, and to a large extent to all losers in hockey? Why does something have to be "wrong" every time a team loses? Please respond, if you dare.

Sincerely,
R&AG
Jackson Heights, New York

––––––––

Dear Marv,

To say I'm getting a bit aggravated with the so-called "professionals" of the NBA is an understatement. This evening I saw a clear violation during your recap of the Bullets-76ers game—a "3-step" Dr. J. move, to the hoop, as usual.

What's going on, anyway? Shuffling of the feet before a drive or jump shot, shifting of pivot feet before a move to the hoop, pushing and shoving underneath, palming of the ball (Mr. Monroe's trick) are all rule violations. I could beat these clowns one-on-one if the refs called the violations.

Why don't you do an in-depth report on this nonsense? Or can't you handle it?

Sincerely,
VB
Staten Island, New York

———

Dear Marv,

I thought you might enjoy hearing how your now famous "Yesss" has influenced my youngest son.

He was six at the time and he was still having some problems disciplining himself to take the time to go to the bathroom.

One day as he was sitting in the bathroom in his normal hurry to get out and play, there was the faint sound of a splash and then the famous "Yesss" from him.

He's almost eight now and still gives the "Yesss" when he's shooting baskets or playing football.

Keep up the good work,
BA
Pequannock, New Jersey

———

Dear Marv,

You're the best sportscaster I ever heard. Please send me two tickets for the Portland-Knicks game next Tuesday night.

Sincerely,
RB
East Williston, New York

Dear Marv,

You lost control in the Jimmy Connors interview. Only kids blow their cool, Marv, not adults. Obviously you dislike Connors. It is not your job to show that, but to report. Also you were rude.

Constructively from
EK
Morristown, New Jersey

---

Dear Marv,

I think it's about time Connors addressed himself to the fact that he's a millionaire because thousands of tennis fans across the world pay good money to see him play. The public should boycott every tournament he participates in. I know I won't pay to see him again. I want to say that I felt you won your match with him, 6-0, 6-0, 6-0.

Keep it up.
DG
Flushing, New York

A young Bob Wolff admits he was given lessons on how to smoke a cigar. In one of his early experiences he says he was pleased with the way he extolled a particular brand—until the sponsor suggested that the next time he should take the wrapper off the cigar before smoking it.

# 12 PUTTING A HEAD ON THE COMMERCIAL

The amber colored liquid splashed evenly into the glass, gradually climbing up the sides with a creamy white head topping it off. It looked absolutely delectable to a beer drinker, which, after all, was exactly the idea. Sportscaster Bob Wolff had worked for weeks on his technique, mastering the speed of his pour so that the liquid landed at just the right angle to build a healthy head. Pouring a glass of beer is no haphazard task for the sportscaster who must sell the brew on television.

Bob was working for the old Washington Senators some years back and in spring training he not only spent his time familiarizing himself with the players but also devoted himself to perfecting his pour. "I had good hands for it," recalled Wolff. "In fact, I was so well drilled that I could pour with either hand and bring the head up just the way the ad agency boys wanted it."

Now came the trip north from the Senator's Florida training base. Each day, Wolff dutifully put in his 30 minutes or so of pouring practice so that by opening day he would be ready. The beer would look so tempting when he poured, that the viewer could all but taste it swimming over his tongue and making its way down his parched throat. Wolff's pour would have them dashing madly through the house in a straight line for the refrigerator and a cold one.

Finally, the Senators arrived home for the traditional presidential opener, a ritual for Washington baseball. The broadcast went off like clockwork, and the Senators even

137

remembered to win—no small accomplishment for them. But if you asked the ad agency, the broadcast had bombed. That's because Wolff made a technical mistake when he was pouring the sponsor's product and the beer splashed over the top of his glass, creating a small calamity in the booth.

"The thing to remember," jokes Wolff, "is that when the One Great Sponsor comes to write against your name, he cares not who won or lost or how well you covered the game. He cares how you poured the beer."

But, let's face it. The sponsor pays the freight and in exchange for the money he's laying out, he's entitled to get his message across, exactly the way he wants it. Some sponsors want their messages delivered by the same broadcasters who are doing the play-by-play of the games. Others hire professional announcers, whose job is to read sponsor-copy. And some sponsors have become broadcasters themselves. Tom Carvel sells his own soft ice cream and Frank Perdue has become a celebrity, courtesy of his chicken advertisements.

On the hockey and basketball radio broadcasts I do, there's about a 50-50 split on the commercials that I read live and the ones that are on tape, either with my voice or a musical jingle or some other material. I really enjoy reading the commercials. It's a challenge to get them in without losing any of the game action. That, of course, is the toughest part—fitting the messages in at the appropriate moment.

On television, fitting in the commercials is the job of the director, who calls all the shots. On radio, with just a play-by-play man, color commentator, statistician, and engineer in the booth, it takes split-second timing to know just when to break for a commercial. I'll cue the commercial with a line like "Back after this," and the engineer will plug in the tape at that moment. When I'm reading live copy, I make a real effort at sincerity. The sponsor has a right to expect that in exchange for the money he's paying. And when I'm through with the spot, I'm careful to simply drop the copy to the floor to get it out of the way. I make sure not to crumple it up. If you've ever heard the sound of paper being crumpled over a microphone and amplified through a radio speaker, you know why I avoid doing that.

Commercial timing has always been a problem in certain sports. Baseball and football have built-in gaps, when it's easy to fit in commercials—baseball, between innings and football, during the automatic timeouts following kickoffs, punts, and during the time it takes players to regroup for the next play. Hockey and basketball, however, don't offer that luxury. Hockey's only play stoppages come when there's a goal, a penalty, or an offsides and you can never be guaranteed of either of those developments. In basketball, teams are forced to take a timeout in order to allow broadcast sponsors time to get in their messages. Those TV timeouts aren't terribly popular with the fans in the arena, who are waiting for the action and don't have beer or automobile commercials to occupy the dead time. Hockey also has TV timeouts, and linesmen wear beepers, attached to their belts, that keep them in touch with the broadcast booth. When the commercial is over, the booth beeps the linesman, signaling him that the puck can be dropped and play resumed. Again, not a terribly popular device for the fans in the building, watching players skate around aimlessly until the linesman gets his beep.

Reading a sponsor's message on radio is one thing, but when I see some of the stuff that baseball play-by-play men have to do on behalf of their clubs, well, that's awfully tough to take. I would have a rough time not spoofing in that situation. I mean, I don't think I could go on the air with a kid sitting next to me wearing a Met or Yankee hat, and seriously read the promotion material that baseball broadcasters have to handle. I'd feel like I was doing a spot for *Saturday Night Live*. It's so corny, and I think the fans know it. But the clubs understandably take it seriously. Fortunately there aren't that many promotions that have to be plugged that way.

I'm not suggesting that sports teams should not take advantage of their broadcasts to plug upcoming events. In fact, you are performing a service by reminding listeners what teams are coming to town for upcoming games. And there's nothing wrong with including special events in those schedule reminders. But there ought to be a limit on how far a broadcaster has to go. He does, after all, have to maintain his believability as an impartial reporter, and shilling for the home team can damage that image. I believe that first and foremost, a sportscaster is a reporter doing over the air what a newspaperman does in print. I think we have to be objective and I resent it strongly when I hear a broadcaster who is an out-and-out homer.

I am in a rather unique position because I serve two functions as a broadcaster. I am both a play-by-play announcer for two teams as well as a sportscaster on a daily TV news program. For some people, that might be a problem because of the conflict between the impartiality of the daily show and the rah-rah homerism of the play-by-play man. The way to avoid the problem is not to be a homer, and I've always been extra careful to slam the Knicks and Rangers when they deserve it, both on the play-by-play game broadcasts and on my daily programs. In fact, I often get mail from viewers and listeners who complain that I don't root enough for my teams. Well, I consider those complaints to be compliments. That's because I try to go the other way—to present a fair and accurate reporting picture of just what's going on. I never want to wear the tag of "homer." And to its credit, the management of Madison Square Garden has never interfered with my approach.

One time I was doing a commentary on my newscast, reporting on the ragged play of the Knicks. The producer felt that the remarks were so strong that he ran a line on the screen, identifying me as the voice of the Knicks. I don't think I'll ever be accused of playing favorites with the teams whose games I broadcast. Sure, I prefer to see the Rangers and Knicks win rather than lose their games. After all, I'm closer with the players and front office personnel of those clubs than I am with the visiting teams'. But my first responsibility is to the listeners and that is to report exactly what is going on, good, bad, or indifferent, regardless of how it reflects on the home team. You can't lie. If you don't say when things are bad, you won't be believed when you say things are good.

Reading commercials for your team is kind of a gray area that lies somewhere between the total impartiality I think a broadcaster should maintain and the "homer" positions that some of them, particularly in baseball, fall into. Your job as a broadcaster is to report the action and capture the excitement which will draw fan interest.

Team and sport loyalty is a two-edged sword, though. While I feel it's unfair for a team to expect its broadcaster to shill, I also think a team has the right to expect that its announcer won't show up on the other side of the street, trying to push a competitive product. Wouldn't it sound ridiculous, for example, if Harry Caray, who broadcasts Chicago White Sox games, went on the air and suggested the fans shoot on over to

Wrigley Field to see the Cubs play, or down to Arlington Park for the horse racing? If Caray is going to be a salesman, he ought to be selling the White Sox. Yet in New York we've seen a similar conflict of interest situation arise over a commercial.

Phil Rizzuto, who has been broadcasting Yankee games for two decades now, popped up on television spots plugging the New York Racing Association and the programs at Belmont Park and Aqueduct Race Track. Part of the copy and the thrust of the advertising campaign identifies thoroughbred racing as "New York's No. 1 spectator sport." That, of course, may be entirely true, but I'm not sure if it was appropriate for Rizzuto to be selling racing, a sport that competes for the same entertainment dollar that baseball goes after. Rizzuto is, after all, a baseball person and a spokesman for a club with which he has a strong, long-term identification.

The NYRA commercial spots raised a few eyebrows around town, both in and out of the broadcast business. If I were Rizzuto, I'd never have done those spots. I think he was wrong to accept the assignment, regardless of whether he had George Steinbrenner's blessing or not. To me it was poor judgment on his part. Would you expect to see jockey Steve Cauthen selling Yankee games? Of course not. And it's just as inappropriate to see the Scooter inviting you to spend a day at the track instead of the ball park.

What it boils down to is that you can't always accept every advertising or commercial spot that is offered. You have to be selective and choose the ones you're going to do with care. I try to limit my involvement to national sponsors and I usually do voice-overs—the narrative that delivers the sponsor's message while something else is happening on the screen.

There is another wrinkle that has developed recently in the commercials and advertising business, and that involves celebrity endorsements of products and the responsibility of the celebrity for the reliability of the products he or she endorses.

If Jimmy Slugger heartily recommends He-Man after shave lotion, and if when you put it on you attract mosquitoes instead of pretty girls, is Mr. Slugger responsible? Maybe. The Federal Trade Commission thinks so. The FTC convinced singer Pat Boone to absorb part of the responsibility for refunds when an acne cream he endorsed didn't do as thorough a job as his commercials promised it would. Shortly after that a woman from California sued actor Karl Malden when her refund for lost American Express Travelers Checks wasn't as speedy as his television spots promised it would be.

The ramifications of those kinds of legal actions are of serious concern and that's why familiar personalities are being extremely careful about the commercials they make these days. The income is nice, but it isn't worth the aggravation of litigation. I don't think, though, that Rizzuto has to worry, unless some bettor who drops a bundle at the track tries to blame it on him.

Sponsors like the celebrity advertisers. They bring instant recognition to a product, and the message contained in the commercial copy is almost secondary. Joe DiMaggio is an automatic identification for Mr. Coffee. In New York, Joe D. is also used by a local bank, the Bowery. His celebrity competition in the New York banking business comes from the Broadway theater community. The Dry Dock Savings Bank uses actress Jane Powell to deliver its messages, while the Emigrant Savings Bank has actor Eli Wallach as it spokesman.

Actors and actresses have often been used in product endorsement and commercial roles, but recently sports personalities have become more popular for these jobs. An actor or actress makes one, perhaps two movies in a year. A sports personality is in the news day-in and day-out—constantly seen by the public. That's why sponsors want those faces and those names for their products.

Nationally, O.J. Simpson with Hertz Rental Cars and Don Meredith with Lipton Tea—and DiMaggio with Mr. Coffee—are good examples of sports personalities who have become permanent spokesmen for particular products. These aren't one-shot commercial pitches. These are long-term deals in which the personalities are used as a regular part of all the client's advertising programs. These deals are the most lucrative, and contracts can pay as much as $250,000 for the term of the agreement. That's superstar money, and it is reserved for the heavyweights of the sports industry. But there's plenty of work for personalities on lower levels as well. There are, for example, the Miller Lite Beer commercials, one of the most successful series of television advertising spots ever conceived.

Attorney Marty Blackman, who represents athletes in contract negotiations and is also retained by sports-minded corporations to do promotional work, had a hand in putting together some of the Miller commercials. The theme of the campaign is to deliver the sponsor's message that the beer is less filling than others and does not sacrifice taste for its lower caloric content. The method used in many of the spots was to put two recognizable sports personalities in conflict over the virtues of Miller Lite.

"Miller Lite had a marketing problem," said Blackman. "They had to make beer drinkers try a new product whose appeal was to be that it was less filling. What was required was a macho campaign that would eliminate any negative image a light beer might create in the consumer's mind. So they turned to sports."

Federal laws prohibit active athletes from endorsing alcoholic beverages. That meant Miller had to go to sports figures who were retired, and thus we saw ex-NFL stars Matt Snell and John Mackey in an arm wrestle; former NBA referee Mendy Rudolph and ex-coach Tom Heinsohn in a tavern debating the same way they had on the basketball court; retired hockey stars Boom Boom Geoffrion and Jacques Plante shouting at each other in French (with appropriate English subtitles); and even New York Yankee owner George Steinbrenner and manager Billy Martin arguing, climaxed by a touch of TV verite that had George tell Billy, "You're fired!" That one was almost too true to life to be used.

"The genius of the Miller campaign is that they used the athletes in humorous situations, not as hard-sell salesmen," said Blackman. "They put the characters in situations that fit their physical attributes or images."

One of the early Miller commercials showed ex-football star Rosey Grier sitting in a rocking chair knitting. He was flanked by two other ex-NFL linemen, Ray Nitschke and Ben Davidson. But only Grier was identified. The others, obviously football types, were referred to as "Rosey's friends." When Miller started getting inquiries about the other two characters, and when people started asking whether Snell or Mackey had won the arm wrestling match, the company and its advertising agency, McCann-Erickson, knew they had reached the public with the spots. By using the characters in plausible, interesting situations instead of trying to make them into pitchmen, the commercials scored.

Filming a commercial like the Miller campaign generally

This was in California, where I got to do NBC-TV "promos" with Dick Van Dyke, among others. (NBC)

takes about one day's time, but it can be extremely rewarding financially. For personalities not quite at the superstar level, commercial spots can pay anywhere from $10,000 to $25,000. And remember, that's for a single day's work.

There has been a continuing debate in the television business over whether news personalities should be permitted to make commercials. The argument presented by the networks and their affiliated stations was that appearances in commercials by their news show people could compromise the individuals involved and that it would shatter their credibility as independent news reporters. Countering that argument was the fact that ABC sports personalities such as Jim McKay, Frank Gifford, and Howard Cosell have been permitted (because of clauses in their individual contracts) to do commercial work with no apparent negative effect on their credibility.

Another factor involved here is that in previous years at NBC, personalities on the *Today* show like Barbara Walters, Hugh Downs, and Gene Shalit not only were allowed to do commercials but, in fact, were required to do them as part of their jobs. NBC claimed that it was okay because they were doing the spots within their own show and thus benefitting their show. But to me, that was hypocritical.

It took a long time but eventually my business agent, Dave Cogan, and I broke down the resistance against having me, a news personality, do commercials. The *Today* precedent and the ABC examples helped and so did the fact that I was already doing them as part of my play-by-play duties on the Rangers and Knicks broadcasts. Eventually, NBC agreed, and after years of turning them down, I've been accepting commercial assignments. And I don't think the change has affected my credibility any more than running through airports for Hertz changes the image of O.J. Simpson to football fans, or brewing coffee makes Joe DiMaggio any different to baseball fans.

Filming *The Fish That Saved Pittsburgh*, I had a chance to play alongside Jonathan Winters, left, and Emmet Walsh.
(LORIMAR PRODUCTIONS)

# 13 THE FISH THAT SAVED PITTSBURGH

Forget the Pirates and Steelers and Penguins. The biggest thing to hit Pittsburgh in recent times was "The Fish" who, we are told, saved the town. I have this bit of information firsthand, because for a dozen days I participated in the filming of a Hollywood production called, appropriately enough, *The Fish That Saved Pittsburgh.*

Lorimar Productions filmed *The Fish*, Hollywood's latest dip into the world of professional basketball. The stars were comedian Jonathan Winters, Stockard Channing, whose credits include *Grease*, and Peter Issacson, who was the second lead to Don Rickles in television's *CPO Sharkey*. The Fish is Julius Erving, whose astrological sign, Pisces, becomes the turning point in the season for a lowly team called the Pittsburgh Pythons. The rest of the film is peopled by familiar pro basketball faces. Dr. J.'s teammates on the Pythons, who later change their names to the Pisces for practical and astrological reasons, include Meadowlark Lemon, the longtime star of the Harlem Globetrotters. Kareem Abdul-Jabbar, Norm Nixon, Lou Hudson, and Connie Hawkins. All play for a fictional Los Angeles team. Bob Lanier is with Detroit and Spencer Haywood, Lonnie Shelton, Butch Beard, and Ticky Burden play for New York.

The film is a fantasy about an awful pro basketball team. The coach, Flip Wilson, quits in disgust. His only halfway-decent player is a million dollar bonus baby, Moses Guthrie, who is played by Julius. The team loses game after game, despite Guthrie's play. Finally, a 12-year-old ball boy figures out the problem. Guthrie is a Pisces, but his inept teammates are not.

**147**

They are astrologically incompatible, and to solve the dilemma, the other players must all be fired and replaced with players born under the sign of Pisces. The scheme is just weird enough to fascinate team owner Winters, who puts it into effect and hires Ms. Channing as the club's resident astrologist. Naturally, the team rallies around the sign of the fish—instead of hot dogs, Winters orders fish sticks sold at the concession stands—and reaches the championship finals. I won't tell you the ending, but it's properly bizarre, fitting the film and everything about it, quite well.

The first thing you learn about the movies is that filmmakers take as long as is necessary to get each shot just right and let the schedule be hanged. I was told that my role would take two-and-a-half days to shoot. I wound up spending close to two weeks in Pittsburgh, most of it standing around, waiting for the shots to be made and remade until the director and producers were satisfied.

Most sports movies are poorly done, with flagrant mistakes and blunders sprinkled throughout. They are Grade B in my book. The Fish, however, is far from that. The producers hired Jerry Tarkanian, the coach at Nevada-Las Vegas, as a technical advisor for the basketball shots. He choreographed the court action. They used a hand-held camera, weighing 75 pounds, to record many of the running plays. It was the same technique used in the Academy Award winning ballet film, The Turning Point.

For each play, the cameraman would run alongside the players, moving with them as he shot. Naturally, as the play moved past the scorer's and announcers' table, the scorer and announcers had to be in position. So even though my role was not being shot at a particular moment, I still had to be on the set, as background decoration. It's attention to little details like that that helps make the production techniques in The Fish a cut above most sports movies I've seen.

When you go to a movie that lasts two- or two-and-a-half hours, it's hard to imagine the shooting of it taking weeks and even months to complete. But that's exactly the way the film business operates. Problems always seem to crop up and The Fish had its share. First, and probably foremost, was attracting fans to the Pittsburgh Civic Arena. You can't have a basketball film without crowds in the stands, and rounding up enough people was one of the major problems for The Fish. The

I never made the movies as a ballboy. That's the role James L. Bond III played in *The Fish That Saved Pittsburgh*. We're with Stockard Channing, the starlet who was the team astrologer in the movie. (LORIMAR PRODUCTIONS)

producers placed ads in the newspapers, offering all kinds of giveaways and attractions to lure fans. Disc jockeys plugged the production on radio, urging people to come to the Civic Arena and play a part in the movie that would place Pittsburgh on the entertainment map. Remember that old movie called, *What If They Gave A War and Nobody Came?* Well, Lorimar and producers Gary Stromberg and David Dashev were giving a movie, and nobody came.

Finally, after a meeting with Mayor Richard Caliguiri during which the producers mentioned the possibility of moving the film to another town, Pittsburgh got behind the project. It became a test of civic pride and on those terms, the city came through. One of the reasons the producers were adamant about wanting to stay in Pittsburgh to make their film was the unique retractable roof that sits on the Civic Arena. In the seventh game of the championship series, the Pisces arrive for the showdown contest via a giant balloon, dropping neatly through the Civic Center roof to the roaring approval of the crowd. When it was time to shoot that scene and the roof was rolled back, guess what kind of weather Pittsburgh was experiencing. If you said rain, you were absolutely right. So filming stopped until the weather cleared and the roof could be retracted without the people inside the arena drowning.

Two of the Pittsburgh-based casting directors for *The Fish* were Clayton Hill and Sharon Cèccatti, who were in charge of hiring extras. Most of the extras were paid $25 per day, though the fee could go to $37 if they were on camera more than others. It's amazing how the movie bug can bite some people. One of the extras they hired was a male nurse who had quit his job so he could spend four or five weeks working on this movie. This was the kind of opportunity that you wouldn't want your job or career to interfere with, I guess.

Hill and Ms. Ceccatti are also part-time actors. Their last big roles were in a film called *Dawn of the Dead,* in which they play the lead zombies. They cast 1,200 zombies all from the Pittsburgh area, for that movie. It is not easy to find 1,200 zombies anyplace, especially in Pittsburgh. Of course, their task was made easier because *Dawn of the Dead* had a major selling point going for it. It is, after all, the sequel to *Night of the Living Dead.*

These are the fascinating little bits of information you pick up on the road to Hollywood fame and fortune. One guy who, I think, may have a difficult time pursuing that road after making his film debut in *The Fish* is Kareem Abdul-Jabbar. Kareem, who almost never gets thumbed out of a basketball game, nearly got himself thrown out of this movie. That is not easy, but Abdul-Jabbar managed it with one of the most awesome displays of temper I've ever seen.

It started during one of those long waits that all of us experienced. Kareem decided to do his waiting in a chair, a move that seemingly made sense. The problem was that the chair he chose happened to be assigned to the cinematographer. Movie folks are very possessive, particularly about their chairs, and the Hollywood man, perhaps not realizing that Abdul-Jabbar is seven-two, 235 pounds, suggested that Kareem park himself someplace else. Apparently, he was not terribly polite about it, either. They exchanged a few unpleasantries and Kareem went on to the court to shoot a scene. But you could almost see the steam escaping from his ears, and anyone who has seen Abdul-Jabbar in action knew that his fuse was lit and an explosion was coming. All during his scene in front of the cameras, Kareem must have been boiling from his exchange with the man from the movie. Finally, when the scene ended and Kareem was walking off the set, he decided to do something about it. He headed straight for the chair in question which, fortunately for its owner, was empty at that particular moment.

With everybody on the set watching him stalk toward it, Abdul-Jabbar had a rapt audience. When he got to the chair, he eyed it for a moment and then spit directly on the seat. Then he picked up the chair, raised it over his head, and smashed it to the floor. That caused the disputed seat to splinter into many small pieces. Having completed his mission, Abdul-Jabbar departed calmly, as if following stage directions that read "exit left."

It was an awesome scene, and director Gilbert Moses bristled. "This can't happen," he said. It was almost as if he was telling Abdul-Jabbar he was out of the movie. For the rest of that day, Barry Nelson, an All-American at Duquesne, subbed for Kareem. It took a monumental peacemaking effort spearheaded by Julius Erving and the producers to bring Abdul-Jabbar back to the set. But he wasn't finished with the controversy.

The movie script called for Pittsburgh's star, played by Erving, to block one of Kareem's famous "sky hook" shots. That was fine until Kareem found out about it. Then, when it came time to film the sequence and they told Abdul-Jabbar what was coming up, he refused to allow it. So it was cut out and the "sky hook"—despite Hollywood and Pittsburgh—remains intact.

Part of the plot called for Meadowlark Lemon, who's about six foot four, to guard Abdul-Jabbar, who stretches some seven feet two inches into the sky. That is obviously a difficult job—that's the way it's supposed to be in the script—and Lemon reacted to it the way so many pro players do. He began pummeling Kareem under the basket. The refs ignored the action because they thought it was part of the script and, to be honest, so did I. But then, when play moved downcourt, Abdul-Jabbar got even with a chop shot that you feel in the stands. By now, it was obvious that the competitive nature of basketball had crept into the film and these two super players—Lemon, who admits to 52, and Abdul-Jabbar, who shatters chairs for exercise—were about to get into a brawl. Again Julius, who ought to qualify for a United Nations' diplomat's job after making this film, calmed it down. It was just a case of basketball players doing what comes naturally and sometimes flareups come naturally. I guess you could call that cinema verité.

The script called for Lemon and Erving to be given the room to do their own particular brands of basketball magic, but sometimes the competitiveness of the players on the court got in the way. On two successive plays, Connie Hawkins blocked shots, which would have been fine except the script called for those shots to go in. So Hawk was taken out of the game, his penalty for being too good at his craft. He realized what he had done and came to the bench laughing.

There is no attempt in the film to identify the Pythons, or Pisces, as an NBA team or for that matter, any of the clubs they play against as members of the NBA. But the producers were careful to cast Abdul-Jabbar with Los Angeles, Lanier with Detroit and Shelton, Haywood, and Beard with New York. They also hired Darell Garretson and Hugh Evans, a couple of NBA officials, to add to the film's realism and authenticity. But Garretson and Evans lasted only 24 hours because they wouldn't live with the script. Part of the story line requires the Pisces to draw out the intermission time between the first and second halves in the championship game for as long as possible. Among the techniques the club uses is to dispatch its cheerleaders to the referees' locker rooms, where they ask the officials for a demonstration of hand-checking on them. When Garretson and Evans heard that, they decided the NBA wouldn't go for it, so they pulled out. Two new, non-NBA referees were imported to take their place and the show, of course, went on.

When the new refs were hired, the producers also remembered to put an extra official at the scorer's table, just the way the NBA does for the playoffs. Those little touches add something extra to this film. Close attention was paid to detail. There was, for example, the matter of my wardrobe. Because I was told that my part would last no more than three days, I packed enough clothes for that much time away from home. There were a couple of changes of slacks and sports jackets. But fortunately, I decided on three identical, pin-striped shirts. That turned out to be a stroke of luck. When I got to Pittsburgh, my first stop was the wardrobe department where my clothes would be selected. They wanted me to look like a sportscaster—not the most difficult assignment in the world. The key, however, was that whatever outfit I chose would be it. There would be no changes. Once we decided on a blue blazer, I was married to that jacket for 11 days. After all, the action was supposed to be a single game. How would it look if I wore a blue blazer in one scene and a brown sports jacket in the next? Sure, we were filming for 11 days but all the action was taking place on a single night. Luckily, I could rotate those pin-striped shirts with the help of the hotel laundry. But the blazer went the distance—with no days off.

The night they rolled back the roof for the grand entrance of the Pisces before the championship game and found the rain falling, we shot until five in the morning. The crowd went the distance. I shot my first speaking part at 4:15 in the morning. I was cast as the network play-by-play announcer for the final game. And again, the crowd went the distance. Once the citizens of Pittsburgh began responding to The Fish, they really got caught up in the making of our movie.

Director Gilbert Moses was the man who controlled the crowds. He needed a full arena for two nights while game action was being shot, and at other times he merely moved the people he had from section to section to suit his needs. Moses was a master. On command, he'd have the fans boo or cheer or laugh. Then he'd have them mouth the same sounds, making the facial expressions without the noise. It was positively eerie sitting in a totally silent arena packed with people who are making a whole series of faces that run the emotional spectrum, but with no sounds whatsoever. Moses' technique was to piece together the necessary sounds and pictures later at the editing stage of the film.

When it came time for me to shoot my role, Moses was right in my face, checking my expressions and emotions. It's not easy to do play-by-play with a Hollywood director sitting a foot away from your nose.

Between them, director Moses whose previous credits include several programs in the Roots series, and producers Stromberg (Car Wash) and Dashev, were determined to put together a high quality film. This was a big budget production and the last 25 minutes are, I think, the best sports scenes and the most expensive ones ever filmed. Part of the action, for example was shot up from beneath a plexiglass floor for an unusual look at the game. That kind of touch is right out of Cecil B. DeMille.

For myself, the memories of The Fish That Saved Pittsburgh will mostly be of sitting or standing around, watching sequences being shot and reshot until the filmmakers were satisfied that the action was perfect. It was quite a different pace from the schedule I follow that keeps me constantly on the run. I enjoyed my role in the movie but, frankly, I'd rather run.

Jim Simpson, with none other than Bob Hope at Super Bowl III, got started in broadcasting at a small, local station. (NBC)

# 14 THE ROAD TO A JOB

It would be wonderful if there was a simple formula that could be applied by every young person who aspires to a career in sportscasting. You know—a list of schools to go to, courses to take, stations to apply at, jobs to start with. But the fact is that this business just isn't that simple. There are as many different directions in which to go as there are young people who want to sit behind microphones. And none of them is right or wrong. No two sportscasters use the same technique to reach their goals, anymore than any two use the same style in their broadcasts. We're all different and so are the roads we've taken in this sometimes crazy business.

There was a time, as recently as the 1950s, when journalism and broadcasting courses were few and far between. What few of them existed were strictly cursory in nature—perhaps a one semester survey course but nothing that treated the subject in any sort of depth. Our field was more or less ignored in the world of academia, and I can understand why. There is no classroom in the world that can teach this business as can the business itself. You learn to broadcast by broadcasting—literally getting behind a microphone and practicing. That technique works even if the microphone is connected to nothing more esoteric than a tape recorder. The point here is that to develop the skills needed to work in radio or television, there is nothing that can teach the craft as well as the craft itself.

Today, though, the academic pendulum has gone the other way. From a time when there were so very few schools offering any courses at all in my field, there now is a wide range of colleges and universities where you can major in communications. It's important to understand that a person who goes to school and majors in journalism or broadcasting is not guaranteed a job. There are hundreds—probably thousands—of young men and women pouring into the market every year, and the business simply cannot absorb them all. Which ones get jobs in communications and which do not often depends on luck. Once you understand that, you'll see how important it is to get yourself in a position where you influence that luck. Sometimes it takes a little aggressiveness like the kind shown by a young man named Larry Baer.

Baer was a political science major at the University of California in Berkeley, and spent his spare time working at the campus radio station. Most schools have stations on campus and for those entertaining professional ambitions, it is absolutely essential that they take advantage of the practical experience available at student-operated facilities. Baer's station was KALX, a 10-watt FM facility that offers no immediate threat to CBS, NBC, or ABC. But it was Baer's station and he was proud of it. So, in the spring of 1977, when the Oakland A's were experiencing some broadcast problems, Baer picked up a telephone and called the owner of the ball club, Charlie Finley.

Among Finley's virtues is the fact that he is an extremely accessible man. Baer reached him with a minimum of difficulty and offered the resources of KALX, all 10 watts worth, to the Oakland ball club. Finley has always admired spunk and originality, and he was rather taken with the idea. But he realized the limitations so small a station would impose on his ball club's broadcasts and turned Baer down. Finley had two weeks left before the start of the season and preferred to gamble on getting a more powerful AM station to beam the A's games. As it turned out, the A's broadcast option for that season was picked up. Still, Baer had planted important seeds for future harvesting. And he would cash in a year later.

In the spring of 1978, the A's were about to be sold and transferred to Denver. Finley seemingly wanted to get out of baseball, once and for all, and oilman Marvin Davis wanted in. The deal seemed set and so, quite understandably, no Oakland radio station planned on broadcasting A's games. Then, less than a week before the start of the season, the sale fell through. The A's would stay in Oakland, at least for the start of the 1978 season. But they would have to do it without a broadcast outlet. Baer called Finley again, and this time, with no place else to turn, Charlie went for the somewhat bizarre idea of having his team's games beamed over a campus station. Larry Baer was in the big leagues.

Finley's deal with KALX covered the first three weeks of the season. Baseball was still trying to put the Denver deal back together, and it was possible the team would move in midstream. Finally the sale collapsed completely and Oakland, for better or worse, was stuck with the A's for another year. At the time, it definitely was for better because the A's got off to a sizzling start and were living in first place. Understandably, they were also attracting considerable listener interest in the Bay Area and there was much radio pounding night after night as KALX's signal drifted in and out. Finally, a more powerful AM outlet contacted Finley and got the club's radio rights. KALX's Cinderella story was over. But Baer's was not. Larry stayed on with the professional crew as part of the production team broadcasting the A's games. He may not stay with it because he had planned on law school before this strange turn of events. But his story is typical of how breaks come in this business, often quite by accident.

Baer's break came because he was working on his campus station. The word to emphasize here is "working." You can take every course in a communications program at a college and university but to really learn this business, you have to work at it. I've found that many courses are too steeped in theory. There is no classroom that can duplicate the real thing. That's why when young people ask me how to get started, I stress that while college is important to their development as well-rounded individuals, working at this craft, certainly at the school station and, of course, elsewhere, if possible, is also vital.

What's important here is placing yourself in a professional broadcasting atmosphere, to get a feel of what a station's operation is really like. You can read textbooks forever and never get that flavor. Don't misunderstand. You can't expect to walk into a station, present yourself to the program director and say, "Here I am." Obviously, it just doesn't work that way. What you have to do is be prepared to take any job, even part-time, just to expose yourself to the atmosphere and to meet people.

Some examples: Dick Enberg's first job in radio came when he was a student at Central Michigan. He was ready to work at the local station as a custodian but was persuaded instead to

Jack Brickhouse, synonymous with the Chicago Cubs, launched his career in Peoria, Illinois. With him here is the Scooter, Yankee broadcaster and former shortstop Phil Rizzuto. (WGN)

apply for the weekend morning disc jockey job—not the most desirable shift. He got the job, and a couple of weeks later when the sports director, who talked him into seeking the DJ spot, left, Enberg got the job and he was on his way.

Jack Brickhouse, voice of the Chicago Cubs, lost a contest but won a career. A radio station in Peoria, Illinois, where he was attending Bradley University, sponsored an audition. There were four prizes and six finalists. Brickhouse finished fifth. He got a job anyway, being allowed to work for two weeks for free. He didn't get any salary, but he had the opportunity to impress some people. And that's more important. After his two-week stint, Brickhouse was hired for $17 per week. "But for that, I also had to double as a switchboard operator," he recalls.

Bob Wolff was a promising baseball prospect, perfecting his skills at Duke University when a broken ankle put him in the broadcast booth instead. When his ankle healed the station offered him full-time employment and Wolff asked his coach, Jack Coombs, for advice. He still was thinking about playing baseball. Coombs advice was, "Keep talking, son." He did.

Another athlete turned broadcaster was Marty Glickman.

Besides his exploits as a runner, which landed him in the 1936 Olympic Games at Berlin, Marty was an outstanding football player as well. And it was a big day on the football field that started Glickman in broadcasting. He had helped Syracuse defeat Cornell, 14-6, scoring both touchdowns. A local businessman was so excited about Glickman's performance that he wanted to put him on radio. Marty was hesitant because he had never thought about broadcasting before, and, in fact, he turned down the idea at first. Then the businessman said $15 per week and a broadcaster was born.

Like Glickman, I went to Syracuse, where local radio stations were willing to give young people a chance. My first chance was on a small FM station, and it was not what you would call a good start for this broadcaster.

I had auditioned at every possible station before I finally got this job as the Saturday morning man, working from 5 A.M. to 1 P.M. The format was classical music, and it was a one-man operation. That included reading the news every hour on the hour. That, of course, was the highlight of my day, because it gave me a chance to read the sports scores. But those other 55 minutes of Mozart, Tchaikovsky, and Beethoven were tough to endure. After playing Chopin and his buddies, I'd belt out five minutes of news in a style that was completely opposite to the character of the station. I was out of my league, and theirs, as well.

I lasted four or five months at the station. Finally the station manager called me in and suggested that we were operating on different wavelengths and that we weren't meant for each other. In other words, I was fired.

It was the first and only time that has ever happened to me, and it was a terrible experience. After all, I was sitting behind a microphone, broadcasting, and had been told that I wasn't right for the job. You think to yourself, maybe this is not for you. It was an ego jolt. How do you explain to your friends and family that you had a job as an announcer, but the station thought you weren't good enough? It hurt, to put it mildly.

But if you bring nothing else to this business, you must bring resiliency—the ability to bounce back from disappointment and start knocking on some more doors. You can't get down on yourself because when you are applying for a job, you are selling yourself. I believed in me and fortunately, so did WOLF, another Syracuse station.

Ray Scott televised the games of Bart Starr and the Green Bay Packers during the fabulous Vince Lombardi years. (CBS)

WOLF had a different format from that FM station. It was rock 'n' roll, the top 40 tunes, music with a beat. The salary was $1 an hour, and I was delighted to get the job. I made the most of it. Together with another disc jockey, "Tricky" Dick Snyder, I promoted record hops. We put up our own money to bring people like Chubby Checker, Dion and the Belmonts, and Bobby Vee (remember them?) for appearances. We would call their agents in New York City, hire the halls, arrange the whole show ourselves. We were real entrepreneurs, and we even made a few bucks.

Then I got the International League's Syracuse Chiefs' baseball play-by-play spot on WFBL and, at the same time, I was keeping busy at the college station, WAER. So I had the entire scope of broadcasting experience while I was in school, and that's so important. When you work on a small station, you do it all. You are not just an announcer. You're often engineer, time salesman, and a few other things—all invaluable experience.

I can't stress too strongly how important it is to take any job you can get when you're starting out, and that means playing classical music at five in the morning if you have to. If you're around a station—no matter what you're doing—you'll meet people and maybe get a shot at a job on the air if one should open up. Getting your foot in the door is very important. My first job on a New York City radio station was as an office boy at WHN. Later, I was the sports director at that same station. The people I met when I was running messages and doing the other chores as an office boy were the same people who hired me to go on the air. If I hadn't been around the station, I might not have gotten that shot.

Circumstances and luck obviously can play a major role. You should remember that there are only a small percentage of on-the-air jobs and breaking into that category is toughest. But there are plenty of behind-the-scenes jobs in production and writing. Don't rule out that kind of work because the new on-the-air personality can be the person who was at the station in some other spot.

The trade journal of our industry is *Broadcasting Magazine*, which carries an extensive classified section listing situations wanted by people in our business. It is read by radio and TV executives, so it is a good idea to advertise yourself. Try not to limit yourself geographically. You never know where you may have to work in that first job. But remember, it is only a first job, a place to start. Think of that first job as a place to gain the experience you must have to get that second or third job and, eventually, the one job you can be happy with.

Often the help wanted ads in *Broadcasting Magazine* will request tapes from applicants. You should routinely record a whole library of these, because stations will demand them when you're under consideration. Keep your tapes short—a total of between five and seven minutes. If you're after a sportscasting job, you'll want a mix on your tape, a sprinkling of play-by-play action (edit it to provide the most exciting moments), a three-minute sports show, complete with commercials, and a minute or so of interview. You want to show that you can handle any sports situation. And it would be a good idea to be able to handle any sport, too. The point is to give yourself as good a chance as you can by showing yourself in a wide variety of activity.

Many popular broadcasters have started small, on local radio stations, gaining valuable experience. People like Ray Scott, Chuck Thompson, Chris Schenkel, and Jim Simpson began their broadcasting careers that way. Danny Gallivan, hockey voice of the Montreal Canadiens, was working in Nova Scotia, doing play-by-play for a junior hockey team, when he got his break. The team played a game in the Montreal Forum and Gallivan, of course, accompanied them there. A Canadiens' official heard his work, made a mental note of the name, and the next thing Gallivan knew, he was doing broadcasts of the Canadiens.

Sometimes the breaks come in strange places. Jim Simpson can tell you about that. Simpson was stationed in Finland with the United States Navy in 1952. The Olympic Games that year were held in Helsinki, and Jim was assigned to cover Navy athletes in the Games. That made him the perfect man when CBS was looking for somebody to provide network feeds. He planned his day so that his freelancing for CBS did not interfere with his Navy duties, and he was able to gain experience and contacts that helped him when he was discharged.

Broadcasters come from diverse backgrounds. Dick Enberg was an assistant professor of health sciences before becoming a full-time broadcaster. Win Elliot owns a degree in zoology. Howard Cosell was an attorney before he was a broadcaster. Cosell's football partners, Frank Gifford and Don Meredith,

Win Elliott graduated from school with a degree in zoology to a varied world of sportscasting. (CBS)

were NFL stars before moving to the broadcast booth. Curt Gowdy was a former college basketball player working as a high school sports reporter on a local newspaper and broadcasting phantom games in the privacy of his room. Chuck

My team: Kenny, Brian, Jackie, wife Benita, and Denise. Denise and Brian are twins. (BRUCE BENNETT)

Thompson began his career as a singer. Don Dunphy was a public relations man. Ray Scott worked for an advertising agency.

The point is that there is no prescribed recipe for getting into this business. We all come from different backgrounds with diverse preparation for our jobs. The road to a seat behind a microphone sometimes takes strange turns. My brother, Al, was a backup goalie for Ohio University when he was getting practical experience, broadcasting their games. The fact that he had to work in pads and skates might seem strange to some people, but not to Alan. My other brother, Steve, found no hockey team at Kent State when he got there. So he was instrumental in the organizing drive for one and wound up as president, traveling secretary, public relations man and, of course, voice of the Kent State Clippers when they were born.

When you go out and look for that first job, you'll find most stations will want somebody with experience. The question is how do you get experience if no one will hire you without it? You have to be persistent, determined to find that station that will accept campus station experience, which you can expand by broadcasting phantom games into a tape recorder. Save your tapes and listen to your technique. Work on improving it and submit the best ones to station managers when you go out looking for that first job.

Part of the solution to the first-job problem is setting your sights on an attainable target. There's nothing wrong with starting at a small station and, in fact, there's plenty right with it. When you take the small-station route you can be sure that you'll learn a lot more at that level simply because there are less people there, and each one has to do more things. You'll constantly be adding to your personal storehouse of talent and ability—qualities that you'll be able to use when it's time to move on to another station.

Auditions are vital. They are the tryouts of our industry, the place where new talent is found. Get as many of these as you can because they provide you with a showcase for yourself, and you never know when you'll click and provide the station with the exact combination of broadcast abilities it is looking for. You might not get the job you're auditioning for but you may make such a good impression that the station people will remember you and call you later on.

It's important when you try out for a job to be yourself. Don't try to sound like anybody except the person you are. Station managers generally are put off by imitations. You must have enough confidence in your own voice to do the job for you. One of the things you have to offer stations is a fresh new sound. Don't be mousetrapped into trying to provide a used, old one in its place.

Like any other job-hunters, there are dos and don'ts for aspiring broadcasters to keep in mind. Do be persistent but don't come on so strong that you turn off potential employers. Do prepare audition tapes, but don't make them interminable. Do get as much practical experience as you can and don't limit yourself, either by the kind of work you'll do or the place you'll do it.

There are scores of schools offering degrees in communications with specialties in broadcasting, and that course of study is certainly recommended here, but I must say that it is by no means required. You can see from the backgrounds of some of the broadcasters we've talked about that my colleagues have widely varied experience. There are full, four-year programs in some schools and shorter, more concentrated plans at specialized schools. But, like Win Elliot, you might study zoology and wind up as a broadcaster. You never know. Life is funny that way.

You should prepare yourself for disappointments because, undoubtedly, you will get turn-downs from stations not willing to give newcomers a chance. But people in this business share a universal dedication that helps them bounce back from those rejections. Remember, if 20 station managers say no, the 21st might not. And he's the one you have to find, the one who will say that magic word—"Yesss!"

Yesss! And it counts! (NBC)

# GLOSSARY

No broadcasting primer would be complete without a glossary defining some of the most commonly used words and phrases which comprise the language of my business. I've listed some of them and tried to explain them, so that when you walk into a newsroom or studio, you'll be able to understand the terms being used. The list is by no means complete, but it does include some of the essential parts of the broadcast dictionary. Some of it is simple and obvious; some of it is jargon which has developed over the years. All of it is important to know if you're involved in the sometimes mysterious world of radio and television.

**Assignment Desk**—Coordinates the assignment of film- and tape-crews to cover news and feature stories. The desk is hooked up to fire and police radios, permitting instant coverage in the case of a breaking news story.

**Billboards**—This is the opening of a program, often combined with a graphic in television and theme music. It introduces the voice of the announcer and the name of the sponsor. For example: "Tonight, from Madison Square Garden, the New York Knicks and the Boston Celtics, brought to you by . . ."

**Board**—The device which sends your signal on the air. Engineers control the board in larger stations, but in smaller stations, announcers become jacks-of-all-trades and control the board along with their other duties.

**Copy**—The script or the story is called copy. I write my own script from wire-service copy (AP, UPI) or my own sources.

**Crawl**—The list of credits, with all those people involved in the production of a television show. Union regulations require that those credits be presented at least once a week and, on network news shows, that is usually done on Fridays.

**Crews**—The team of television technicians sent into the field to film or tape a news event or interview. In film, a three-person crew is used at NBC—one person handling the camera, a second, who is a lighting technician, and the third for audio. For tape, a two-person crew is used. The camera person also handles lighting. Of course, at smaller stations one person often does it all.

**Cues**—In a studio, when the stage manager points to the on-screen talent to indicate that he is on the air, he is said to be giving a cue. In addition, there are In-Cues and Out-Cues. An In-Cue on a film or tape story will be the first few spoken words of that segment. Leading into that piece, the announcer will use the In-Cue in writing his narration copy. The Out-Cue is the last few words of the segment which gives the director in the control room knowledge of when the piece is ending. He can then time his switch back to the live camera.

**Director**—The one who controls the technical aspects of the show. The director usually has a selection of camera shots from which to choose. He selects the picture seen at home.

**Dissolve**—Used for a transition from one camera to another, with a slight overlapping of the two pictures.

**Dolly**—A piece of equipment on which a camera is mounted, providing movement and allowing the camera to follow the action rather than remain stationary.

**Edit**—In radio and television, editing is the process of refining material for broadcast, and selecting what is to be presented on the air. We edit film by looking at it on a monitor and selecting what we want to show.

**Electronic Journalism**—The use of electronic equipment to cover news events via video tape and electronic cameras. NBC calls this process "EJ," although other networks have different terminology for the same technique.

**Fade-In and Fade-Out**—Fade-in is the TV director's parlance for the change or switch from black to picture. Fade-out is for the change or switch from picture to black.

**Graphics**—Artwork utilized as a background. Sometimes graphics are created by artists. At other times pictures are used.

Often a graphic will be composed of something as simple as a wire-service basketball or football poll, listing the top five teams in the country.

**Isolation**—Having a camera follow one player, like a wide receiver in a football telecast. Sometimes the isolation will be on a matchup in the line which might not be noticed otherwise. Isolation adds an extra dimension to coverage.

**Log**—The programming list for the day. A broadcaster must sign his programming log each day, listing the time each commercial is aired. This is an FCC regulation.

**Mini-Cams**—Hand-held cameras used to provide unique closeup shots never before available. Usually used in spot-news coverage, although NBC's NewsCenter4 has begun using them in the studio to provide a different look on the screen.

**Mobile Unit**—In coverage of a sports event, there is a production truck parked outside the stadium where technicians put together the total telecast package. This truck is called the mobile unit.

**Producer**—The one responsible for the content and talent decisions on what goes on the air.

**Promo**—Short for promotion. When the anchorman says "Sports is next after these messages . . ." that's a promo. Those recorded spots for sports or news are also called promos.

**Remote**—Any broadcast away from a studio, providing a live pickup, either in sports or news, is called a remote.

**Replay**—A second look at a play, often in slow motion. Sometimes sports coverage will include repeated replays on the same piece of action, especially if it is a controversial call.

**Seven-Second Delay**—The built-in protection for radio talk shows which permits the station to prevent anything it does not wish broadcast from going out over the air. The delay means that the material being broadcast can be screened by the station before reaching the air.

**Slow Motion or Slow Mo**—Reducing the speed of the action on the replay so that it is clearer to the viewer.

**Station Break**—Identification of the station by its call letters. East of the Mississippi River, all station call letters begin with "W" while west of the Mississippi, they start with "K." There is one exception to that rule. KDKA in Pittsburgh was the first commercial station, and thus was allowed to keep its call letters for the sake of tradition.

**Story Boards**—Frame by frame assembly showing the picture and narration matchup for a commercial.

**Stretch**—The signal given to the on-camera personality when a segment is running short and the production requires that it be extended. Sometimes that happens because the ensuing tape or commercial is not ready to be shown.

**Super**—Placing a name on the screen for identification purposes. Also called super imposing.

**Take One; Take Two**—Switching directions from the director to the technical crew, changing the on-air picture from one camera to another. Each camera has a designated number and the director decides which numbered camera's picture to "take."

**Talent**—On-air personalities.

**Unit Manager**—The individual who oversees the costs and logistics (talent, crews, etc.) for out-of-town telecasts. This includes arranging for travel and hotel accommodations.

**Voice Over**—In a commercial, when the announcer is not on camera, he is said to be doing a "voice over." When the announcer is narrating some film footage, it is also a voice over.

**Wipe**—Changing the on-air picture by means of having it move off to the right, "pushed" in that direction by the new one, which appears from the left. The new picture "wipes" the old off the screen.

# APPENDIX

The following schools, listed by state, are institutional members of the Broadcast Education Association, 1771 N St., N. W., Washington, D. C. 20036. They all offer courses in communications. Many have their own radio stations and some have TV facilities as well.

## ALABAMA

**\*\*Gadsden State Junior College**

Prof. Donald Smith
Dept. of Broadcast Technology
Gadsden State Junior College
Gadsden, Alabama 35903

**Alabama, University of**

Prof. W. Knox Hagood
Dept. of Broadcast & Film Communication
University of Alabama
Drawer D
University, Alabama 35486

## ALASKA

**\*\*Alaska, University of**

Chairman
Dept. of Speech, Drama & Radio
University of Alaska
College, Alaska 99701

\*\* Associate Members

## ARIZONA

**Arizona State University**

Dr. Joe W. Milner
Chairman
Arizona State University
Mass Communications
Tempe, Arizona 85281

**Arizona, University of**

Prof. Frank Barreca
Head, Dept. of Radio-TV
University of Arizona
Tucson, Arizona 85721

## ARKANSAS

**Arkansas State University**

Arkansas State University
Drawer 4-B
State University, Arkansas 72467

**\*\*Arkansas at Little Rock, University of**

Prof. David Guerra
Dept. of Radio-TV-Film
Univ. of Arkansas at Little Rock
33rd & University Avenue
Little Rock, Arkansas 72204

**\*\*John Brown University**

Prof. Ralph C. Kennedy
Director of Communications
John Brown University
Siloam Springs, Arkansas 72761

**CALIFORNIA**

**California State University— Fullerton**

Dr. George A. Mastroianni
Department of Communications
Calif. State University, Fullerton
Fullerton, California 92634

**California State University— Long Beach**

Dr. Robert G. Finney
Chairman
Dept. of Radio-TV
Calif. State Univ., Long Beach
1250 Bellflower Blvd.
Long Beach, Califoria 90840

**California State University— Northridge**

Dr. Bertram Barer
Head, Radio-TV
Calif. State Univ., Northridge
18111 Nordhoff Street
Northridge, California 91324

**California State University— Sacramento**

Prof. Roger L. Walters
Broadcasting Coordinator
Calif. State Univ., Sacramento
UPO 4195

6000 Jay Street
Sacramento, California 95819

**California State University— San Jose**

Dr. Clarence E. Flick
Supervisor, Radio-TV
Theatre Arts Dept.
Calif. State Univ., San Jose
San Jose, California 95192

**\*\*Los Angeles City College**

Radio-TV-Film Department
Prof. Donald T. McCall
Los Angeles City College
855 North Vermont Avenue
Los Angeles, California 90029

**\*\*Moorpark College**

Dr. Al Miller
Chairman
Dept. of Telecommunications
Moorpark College
7075 Campus Road
Moorpark, California 93021

**San Diego State University**

Prof. Kenneth K. Jones
Telecomunications & Film
San Diego State University
5402 College Avenue
San Diego, California 92115

**\*\*San Francisco, City College of**

Prof. Henry Leff, Director
Broadcasting Department
City College of San Francisco
Ocean & Phelan Avenues
San Francisco, California 94112

**San Francisco State University**

Dr. Stuart Hyde, Chairman
Broadcast Communication Arts
San Francisco State University
1600 Holloway Avenue
San Francisco, California 94132

**Southern California, University of**

School of Journalism
University of Southern California
University Park
Los Angeles, California 90007

**Stanford University**

Dr. Henry Breitrose
Department of Communications
Stanford University
Stanford, California 94305

**COLORADO**

**Colorado State University**

Dr. Robert MacLauchlin
Dept. of Speech & Theatre Arts
Colorado State University
Fort Collins, Colorado 80521

**Colorado, University of**

Prof. Harold E. Hill
Department of Communications
University of Colorado
Boulder, Colorado 80302

**Denver, University of**

Dr. Harold Mendelsohn
Chairman
Dept. of Mass Communications
University of Denver
Denver, Colorado 80210

**CONNECTICUT**

**\*\*Bridgeport, University of**

Prof. Howard B. Jacobson
Chairman
Journalism Department
University of Bridgeport
Bridgeport, Connecticut 06602

**DELAWARE**

**\*\*Delaware, University of**

Dr. George Borden, Chairperson
Dept. of Speech/Communications
201 Elliott Hall
University of Delaware
Newark, Delaware 19711

**DISTRICT OF COLUMBIA**

**American University**

Dr. Robert O. Blanchard
Chairman
Department of Communications
American University
Washington, D. C., 20016

**FLORIDA**

**Florida A&M University**

Dr. James Hawkins
Dept. of Journalism
Florida A&M University
Tallahassee, Florida 32307

**\*\*Florida Atlantic University**

Director
Dept. of Communications
Florida Atlantic University
Boca Raton, Florida 33431

**\*\*Florida Technological University**

Dr. M. D. Meeske
Department of Communications
Florida Technological University
Box 25000
Orlando, Florida 32816

**Florida, University of**

Dr. Kenneth A. Christiansen
Director of Television
University of Florida
234 Stadium
Gainesville, Florida 32601

**South Florida, University of**

Prof. Manny Lucoff
Sequence Head, Broadcasting
Dept. of Mass Communications
University of South Florida
Tampa, Florida 33620

## GEORGIA

**\*\*Georgia State University**

Prof. Edward G. Luck
Department of Journalism
Georgia State University
33 Gilmer Street, S. E.
Atlanta, Georgia 30303

**Georgia, University of**

Dr. Worth McDougald
Head, Radio-TV-Film
Henry W. Grady School of Journalism
University of Georgia
Athens, Georgia 30601

## HAWAII

**Hawaii, University of**

Dr. Richard Spingola
Dept. of Speech-Communications
University of Hawaii
2560 Campus Road
Honolulu, Hawaii 96822

## IDAHO

**Idaho, University of**

Art Hooks
Associate Professor of Communications
University of Idaho
Moscow, Idaho 83843

## ILLINOIS

**\*\*Eastern Illinois University**

Jack C. Rang
Director of Mass Communications
Department of Speech
Eastern Illinois University
Charleston, Illinois 61920

**Illinois, University of**

Department of Radio-Television
c/o Theodore Peterson, Acting Head
119 Gregory Hall
University of Illinois
Urbana, Illinois 61801

**\*\*Illinois, University of at Chicago Circle**

Dr. R. V. Harnack
Dept. of Speech & Theatre
College of Liberal Arts
Univ. of Illinois at Chicago Circle
Box 4348
Chicago, Illinois 60680

**Loyola University of Chicago**

Dr. Robert Pirsein, Chairman
Communication Arts Dept.
Loyola University of Chicago
Lewis Towers—820 North Michigan Ave.
Chicago, Illinois 60611

**North Central College**

Herbert R. Nestler
Director of Broadcasting
North Central College
30 North Brainard Street
Naperville, Illinois 60540

**Northern Illinois University**

Dr. Jon T. Powell
Dept. of Speech Communications
Northern Illinois University
DeKalb, Illinois 60115

## Northwestern University

Dr. Stephen May
Dept. of Radio-TV-Film
School of Speech
Northwestern University
Evanston, Illinois 60201

## **Parkland College

Prof. Edward G. Kelly
Parkland College
2400 West Bradley Avenue
Champaign, Illinois 61820

## Southern Illinois University

Department of Radio-Television
c/o Charles T. Lynch
Southern Illinois University
Carbondale, Illinois 62901

## Southern Illinois University, Edwardsville

John A. Regnell, Chairman
Dept. of Mass Communications
Southern Illinois Univ., Edwards-
  ville
Box 73—SIU-E
Edwardsville, Illinois 62025

## **Western Illinois University

Dr. William L. Cathcart
Head
Radio-TV Division
Dept. of Speech & Dramatic Art
Western Illinois University
Macomb, Illinois 61455

## INDIANA

### Ball State University

Dr. William H. Tomlinson
Director
Center for Radio & Television
Ball State University
Muncie, Indiana 47306

## Butler University

Prof. James R. Phillippe
Chairman
Dept. of Radio & Television
Butler University
46th Street at Clarendon Road
Indianapolis, Indiana 46207

## **Evansville, University of

Director
Center for the Study of Communi-
  cations
University of Evansville
P. O. Box 329
Evansville, Indiana 47702

## Indiana State University

Dr. Joe T. Duncan
Director of Broadcasting
Department of Speech
Indiana State University
Terre Haute, Indiana 47809

## Indiana University

Dr. Charles Sherman
Acting Chairman
Dept. of Telecommunications
Indiana University
Bloomington, Indiana 47401

## **Notre Dame, University of

Harry J. Kevorkian
Adjunct Asst. Prof.
American Studies
University of Notre Dame
Notre Dame, Indiana 46556

## DePauw University

Dr. John R. Bittner
Communication Arts & Sciences
DePauw University
Greencastle, Indiana 46135

**Purdue University**

Dean David Berg
Dept. of Communications
Heavilon Hall
Purdue University
West Lafayette, Indiana 47907

**\*\*Vincennes University**

Mark R. Lange
Director of Broadcasting
Department of Broadcasting
Vincennes University
1002 North First Street
Vincennes, Indiana 47591

**IOWA**

**Iowa, The University of**

Dr. Robert Pepper
Associate Head, Broadcasting
Division of Broadcasting/Film
The University of Iowa
102 Old Armory
Iowa City, Iowa 52242

**KANSAS**

**\*\*Fort Hays Kansas State College**

Prof. Jack R. Heather
Director
Radio-TV-Film
Fort Hays Kansas State College
Hays, Kansas 67601

**Kansas State University**

Chairman
Department of Journalism
Kedzie 104
Kansas State University
Manhattan, Kansas 66506

**Kansas, University of**

Dr. Bruce A. Linton
Chairman
Radio-TV-Film
217 Flint Hall

University of Kansas
Lawrence, Kansas 66044

**Washburn University of Topeka**

Dr. Dale N. Anderson
Director of ETV
Washburn University of Topeka
17 and College
Topeka, Kansas 66621

**Wichita State University**

Dr. Frank Kelly
Wichita State University
KMUW Radio
1751 N. Fairmount
Wichita, Kansas 67208

**KENTUCKY**

**\*\*Ashland Community College**

Mr. Bill Sadler
Ashland Community College
1400 College Drive
Ashland, Kentucky 41101

**Eastern Kentucky University**

Mr. James S. Harris
Chairman
Department of Communications
Eastern Kentucky University
Richmond, Kentucky 40475

**Kentucky, University of**

Chairman
Department of Telecommunica-
tions
University of Kentucky
Lexington, Kentucky 40506

**Morehead State University**

Dr. Richard Bayley
Coordinator, Radio-TV
Division of Communication in the
School of Humanities
Morehead State University
Morehead, Kentucky 40351

**Murray State University**

Dr. R. H. McGaughey, Chairman
Dept. of Journalism & Radio-TV
Murray State University
Murray, Kentucky 42071

**Western Kentucky University**

Dr. Randall Capps
Department Head
Dept. of Communications &
  Theatre
Western Kentucky University
Bowling Green, Kentucky 42101

**LOUISIANA**

**Grambling State University**

Dr. Allen Williams
Director of Broadcasting
KGRM
Grambling State University
Grambling, Louisiana 71245

**\*\*Louisiana State University**

Dr. John H. Pennybacker
Department of Speech
Louisiana State University
Baton Rouge, Louisiana 70803

**\*\*Loyola University**

Dr. William M. Hammel
Department of Communications
Loyola University
6363 St. Charles Street
New Orleans, Louisiana 70118

**\*\*McNeese State University**

Prof. David Rigney
Director of Television
Department of Speech
McNeese State University
Lake Charles, Louisiana 70601

**\*\*Northeast Louisiana University**

Dr. V. Jackson Smith

Director of Broadcasting
KNLU Radio
Northeast Louisiana University
Monroe, Louisiana 71201

**Southwestern Louisiana, University of**

Prof. Bernard W. Crocker
Department of Speech
Univ. of Southwestern Louisiana
P. O. Box 4-2091
Lafayette, Louisiana 70504

**MAINE**

**Maine, University of**

Dr. Saul N. Scher
265 Stevens Hall
University of Maine
Orono, Maine 04473

**MARYLAND**

**College of Notre Dame of Maryland**

Sister Sharon Dei, Director
Communication Arts Program
College of Notre Dame of Maryland
4701 N. Charles St.
Baltimore, Maryland 21210

**\*\*Community College of Baltimore**

Prof. Frank Holston, Jr.
Radio-Television
Community College of Baltimore
2901 Liberty Heights Avenue
Baltimore, Maryland 21215

**Maryland, University of**

Dr. Donald Kirkley
Director
Radio-TV Division
Dept. of Speech & Dramatic Arts
University of Maryland
College Park, Maryland 20742

## **Towson State College

Prof. John L. Mackerron
Communication Arts & Sciences
Towson State College
Baltimore, Maryland 21204

## MASSACHUSETTS

### Boston University

Dr. Robert R. Smith
Chairman
School of Public Communications
Boston University
640 Commonwealth Avenue
Boston, Massachusetts 02215

### Emerson College

Prof. Charles E. Phillips
Chairman
Dept. of Broadcasting
Emerson College
130 Beacon Street
Boston, Massachusetts 02116

### **Endicott College

Prof. M. Eileen Kneeland
Chairman
Department of Radio-TV
Endicott College
Beverly, Massachusetts 01915

### Massachusetts, University of

Dr. Kenneth L. Brown
Chairman
Dept. of Communication Studies
University of Massachusetts
Amherst, Massachusetts 01002

### **Mount Wachusett Community College

Prof. Vincent S. Lalenti
Coordinator of Public Communications Curriculum
Mount Wachusett Community College
Gardner, Massachusetts 01440

## MICHIGAN

### Central Michigan University

Dr. Peter B. Orlik, Head
Broadcast & Cinematic Arts Area
Dept. of Speech and Drama
Central Michigan University
Mt. Pleasant, Michigan 48858

### **Delta College

Mr. William J. Ballard
Station Manager, WUCM-TV
Delta College
Delta Road
University Center, Michigan 48710

### Detroit, University of

Dr. Charles A. Dause, Chairman
Communication Studies Dept.
University of Detroit
3800 Puritan
Detroit, Michigan 48221

### **Eastern Michigan University

Prof. William V. Swisher
Director of Broadcasting
Dept. of Speech & Dramatic Arts
Eastern Michigan University
Ypsilanti, Michigan 48197

### **Ferris State College

Robert Willison
Instructor
Electrical/Electronics Dept.
Ferris State College
School of Technical & Applied Arts
Big Rapids, Michigan 49307

### Michigan State University

Dr. Robert Schlater, Chairman
Department of TV-Radio
College of Communication Arts
Michigan State University
East Lansing, Michigan 48823

**Michigan, University of**

Dr. Edgar E. Willis
Department of Speech
University of Michigan
Ann Arbor, Michigan 48104

**\*\*Northern Michigan University**

Dr. George Lott
WNMU-TV
Learning Resources Center
Northern Michigan University
Marquette, Michigan 49855

**\*\*St. Clair County Community College**

Prof. Donna R. Williams
TV Coordinator
St. Clair County Community College
323 Erie Street
Port Huron, Michigan 48060

**Western Michigan University**

Dr. Jules Rossman
Dept of Communication Arts & Sciences
Western Michigan University
Kalamazoo, Michigan 49001

**MINNESOTA**

**Bemidji State College**

Mr. R. K. Smith
Chairman
Department of Communication
Bemidji State College
Bemidji, Minnesota 55601

**Minnesota, University of**

Prof. Leonard D. Bart
Director of Radio-TV
Dept. of Speech & Theatre Arts
University of Minnesota
Minneapolis, Minnesota 55455

**Minnesota, University of— Duluth**

Dan H. Johnson
Instructor
Dept. of Speech Communication
University of Minnesota-Duluth
Duluth, Minnesota 55812

**MISSISSIPPI**

**\*\*Mississippi State University**

Dr. Robert G. Anderson
Professor of Communications
Speech Department
Mississippi State University
P. O. Drawer NJ
Mississippi State, Mississippi 39762

**Mississippi University For Women**

Dr. David P. Kintsfather, Jr.
Dept. Head
Dept. of Journalism & Broadcasting
Mississippi University For Women
Columbus, Mississippi 39701

**Mississippi, University of**

Richard B. Haynes
Director
Division of Radio & Television
Fine Arts Center
University of Mississippi
University, Mississippi 38677

**Southern Mississippi, University of**

Dr. James Hall, Chairman
Department of Radio-TV-Film
University of Southern Mississippi
Box 5141
Hattiesburg, Mississippi 39401

## MISSOURI

### Central Missouri State University

Dr. David Eshelman
Dept. of Mass Communications
Central Missouri State University
Warrensburg, Missouri 64093

### Evangel College

Department of Communications
Evangel College
1111 N. Glenstone
Springfield, Missouri 65802

### **Lindenwood College

Robert G. White
Director of Broadcasting
Broadcast/Journalism Dept.
Lindenwood College
St. Charles, Missouri 63301

### Missouri, University of

Dr. David Dugan
Chairman
Department of Broadcasting
School of Journalism—106 Neff
Hall
University of Missouri
Columbia, Missouri 65201

### Missouri, University of—Kansas City

Dr. Sam Scott, Chairman
Dept. of Communication Studies
University of Missouri-Kansas
City
5100 Rockhill Road
Kansas City, Missouri 64110

### Northwest Missouri State University

J. Robert Craig
Assistant Professor of Speech and
Theatre
Northwest Missouri State University
Maryville, Missouri 64468

### **Park College

Prof. Lowell A. Connor
Director of Media
Communication Arts Department
Park College
Suburban Kansas City, Missouri
64152

### **St. Louis University

Prof. Charles P. Paterson
Department of Speech
St. Louis University
15 North Grand
St. Louis, Missouri 63103

## MONTANA

### **Eastern Montana College

Anneke-Jan Boden
General Manager, KEMC
Dept. of Speech Communications
and Theatre Arts
Eastern Montana College
Billings, Montana 59101

### **Montana State University

Film & TV Department
Montana State University
Bozeman, Montana 59715

### Montana, University of

Prof. Phillip J. Hess
Director
Radio-TV Studios
University of Montana
Missoula, Montana 59801

## NEBRASKA

### Creighton University

Heather Harden
Creighton University
2500 California Street
Journalism & Mass Communications Department
Omaha, Nebraska 68178

**Nebraska, University of— Lincoln**

Dr. Larry Walklin
Television-Radio-Film
School of Journalism
University of Nebraska-Lincoln
253 Avery
Lincoln, Nebraska 68508

**Nebraska, University of— Omaha**

Dr. Mary E. Williamson
Department of Speech
University of Nebraska-Omaha
Box 688, Downtown Station
Omaha, Nebraska 68101

**NEVADA**

**\*\*Nevada, University of**

Prof. Wendell H. Dodds
Radio-TV Center
University of Nevada
106 College of Education
Reno, Nevada 89507

**NEW JERSEY**

**Seton Hall University**

Dr. Al Paul Klose
Chairman
Department of Communication
Seton Hall University
South Orange, New Jersey 07079

**NEW MEXICO**

**\*\*New Mexico State University**

Dr. Frank F. Hash, Head
Dept. of Journalism & Mass Com-
munications
New Mexico State University
Las Cruces, New Mexico 88003

**NEW YORK**

**Brooklyn College**

Dr. Robert C. Williams
Chairman
Dept. of Radio & Television
Brooklyn College
Brooklyn, New York 11210

**\*\*Canisius College**

Dr. W. J. Howell, Jr.
Chairman
Dept. of Communications
Canisius College
2001 Main Street
Buffalo, New York 14208

**\*\*Hofstra University**

Dr. George N. Gordon
Chairman
Communications Arts Dept.
Director, Communications Ctr.
Hofstra University
1000 Fulton Avenue
Hempstead, New York 11550

**Ithaca College**

Dr. Dana R. Ullofh
Chairperson
Television-Radio Department
School of Communications
Ithaca College
Ithaca, New York 14850

**Herbert H. Lehman College**

Dr. Frank Kahn
Director, Mass Communications
Herbert H. Lehman College
Bedford Park Blvd. West
Bronx, New York 10468

**New York University**

Undergraduate Film & TV
School of the Arts
Institute of Film & TV
New York University
South Building, Room 65
Washington Square
New York, New York 10003

**\*\*Niagara University**

Prof. Bruce R. Powers
Director
Communication Studies Program
Niagara University
Lewiston Road
Niagara, New York 14109

**\*\*Queens College**

Dr. Gary Gumpert
Department of Communications
Queens College
Flushing, New York 11367

**St. John Fisher College**

Mr. Thomas P. Proietti
Director, Media Center
Chairman, Communications
Dept.
St. John Fisher College
3690 East Avenue
Rochester, New York 14618

**St. John's University**

Prof. Martin J. Healey
Director, Public Relations
St. John's University
Jamaica, New York 11439

**St. Lawrence University**

Prof. Richard D. Hutto
Public Radio Station WSLU-
FM/Radio-TV Dept.
St. Lawrence University
Canton, New York 13617

**\*\*State University College at Fredonia**

Dr. John Malcolm
Director of Instructional Re-
sources Ctr.
State Univ. College at Fredonia
Fredonia, New York 14063

**State Univ. of New York—Brockport**

Dr. Melvin Smagorinsky
Director
Educational Communications
Center
State Univ. of New York—Brock-
port
Brockport, New York 14420

**\*\*State University of New York—Oswego**

Dr. Lewis B. O'Donnell
Coordinator Radio-TV
Communication Studies Depart-
ment
State Univ. of New York-Oswego
Oswego, New York 13126

**Syracuse University**

Dr. Lawrence Myers, Jr.
Radio & TV Center
Syracuse University
Syracuse, New York 13210

**NORTH CAROLINA**

**Appalachian State University**

Dr. Jon E. Currie
Director of Broadcasting
Dept. of Communication Arts
Appalachian State University
Boone, North Carolina 28608

**\*\*Duke University**

Prof. Joseph Wetherby
Department of English
Duke University
Durham, North Carolina 27706

**\*\*North Carolina State University**

Dr. William G. Franklin, Head
Dept. of Speech Communication
North Carolina State University
Box 5308
Raleigh, North Carolina 27607

**North Carolina, University of**

Prof. A. Richard Elam
Chairman
Dept. of Radio-TV Film
Communication Center
University of North Carolina
Chapel Hill, North Carolina
27514

**\*\*Wilkes Community College**

Al G. Stanley, Instructor
Department of Radio-TV
Wilkes Community College
P. O. Box 120
Wilkesboro, North Carolina
28697

**NORTH DAKOTA**

**North Dakota, University of**

Prof. David E. Beach
Director of Radio
University of North Dakota
Grand Forks, North Dakota
58201

**OHIO**

**Akron, University of**

Dr. William Steis
Dept. of Speech & Theatre Arts
University of Akron
Akron, Ohio 44301

**Bowling Green State University**

Dr. Robert K. Clark
School of Speech Communica-
tion
Bowling Green State University
Bowling Green, Ohio 43402

**\*\*Capital University**

Dr. Armin Langholz
Department of Speech
Capital University
Columbus, Ohio 43209

**\*\*Dayton, University of**

Prof. George C. Biersack
Chairman and Director
Department of Communication
Arts
University of Dayton
300 College Park
Dayton, Ohio 45409

**Denison University**

Prof. Bruce Markgraf
Dept. of Speech Communication
Denison University
Granville, Ohio 43023

**Kent State University**

Dr. John C. Weiser
Coordinator
Division of Telecommunications
Kent State University
Kent, Ohio 44242

**Miami University**

Dr. Ernest E. Phelps
Director of Telecommunications
Miami University
Oxford, Ohio 45056

**Ohio State University**

Dr. Joseph M. Foley
Department of Communication
Ohio State University
154 N. Oval Drive
Columbus, Ohio 43210

**Ohio University**

Dr. Charles E. Clift
Assistant Professor
School of Radio-TV
Ohio University
Athens, Ohio 45701

## **Wright State University

Dr. William C. Lewis
Director Telecommunications
Dept.
Wright State University
Dayton, Ohio 45435

## OKLAHOMA
### **Central State University

Dr. Jack Deskin
Dept. of Oral Communications
Central State University
Edmond, Oklahoma 73034

### Langston University

Joy Flasch
Communication Department
Langston University
P. O. Box 967
Langston, Oklahoma 73050

### **Oklahoma State University

Dr. James W. Rhea
Room 206
Communications Building
Oklahoma State University
Stillwater, Oklahoma 74074

### Tulsa, University of

Prof. Thomas Bohn
Director of Radio & Television
University of Tulsa
600 South College
Tulsa, Oklahoma 74104

## OREGON
### **Blue Mountain Community College

Prof. Blaine T. Hanks
Chairman
Broadcasting Department
Blue Mountain Community
  College
P. O. Box 100
Pendleton, Oregon 97801

### Oregon, University of

Dr. John R. Shepherd
Division of Broadcast Services
University of Oregon
Eugene, Oregon 97403

### **Southern Oregon College

Prof. Ronald Kramer
Director
Broadcast Activities
Southern Oregon College
1250 Siskiyou Blvd.
Ashland, Oregon 97520

## PENNSYLVANIA

### Annenberg, The School of Communications

Dean George Gerbner
Department of Communications
The Annenberg School of Communications
3620 Walnut Street
Philadelphia, Pennsylvania
  19104

### Duquesne University

Dr. Nancy C. Jones
Chairperson
Department of Journalism
Duquesne University
Pittsburgh, Pennsylvania 15219

### **Elizabethtown College

Prof. Donald E. Smith
Chairman
Communication Arts Department
Elizabethtown College
Elizabethtown, Pennsylvania
  17022

**\*\*Northampton County Area Community College**

Kent Kjellgren
Telecommunications Coordinator
Dept. of Speech & Theatre
Northampton County Area Community College
3835 Green Pond Road
Bethlehem, Pennsylvania 18017

**Pennsylvania State University**

Harold E. Nelson
General Manager, WDFM
310 Sparks Building
Pennsylvania State University
University Park, Pennsylvania 16802

**\*\*Pennsylvania State University —Wilkes Barre**

Prof. Ralph E. Carmode, Chairman
Department of Communications
Pennsylvania State Univ.—Wilkes Barre
P. O. Box 1830
Wilkes Barre, Pennsylvania 18708

**Shippensburg State College**

Mr. Richard M. Warner
Dept. of Communication/Journalism
Shippensburg State College
Shippensburg, Pennsylvania 17257

**Temple University**

Prof. Gordon L. Gray
Chairman
Radio-TV-Film
School of Communications & Theatre
Temple University
Philadelphia, Pennsylvania 19122

**\*\*Villanova University**

Prof. R. G. Wilke
Department of Speech
Villanova University
Villanova, Pennsylvania 19085

**\*\*Westminster College**

Prof. Mark C. Klinger, III
Director of Broadcasting
Department of Speech & Drama
Westminster College
New Wilmington, Pennsylvania 16142

## SOUTH CAROLINA

**South Carolina, University of**

Dr. Richard M. Uray
Director
Broadcasting Sequence
School of Journalism
University of South Carolina
Columbia, South Carolina 29208

## SOUTH DAKOTA

**Black Hills State College**

Richard Boyd
Assistant Professor-Communications
Black Hills State College
1200 University
Spearfish, South Dakota 57783

**\*\*South Dakota State University**

Eric Brown
Director of Educational Media
South Dakota State University
Brookings, South Dakota 57006

## South Dakota, University of

Chairman
Department of Communications
University of South Dakota
Vermillion, South Dakota 57069

## TENNESSEE

## **Jackson State Community College

J. Charles Cooper
Coordinator of Instructional
  Media
Jackson State Community College
Box 2467
Jackson, Tennessee 38301

## Memphis State University

Prof. Marvin R. Bensman
Director of Broadcasting-Film
Department of Drama & Speech
Memphis State University
Memphis, Tennessee 38111

## **Southern Missionary College

Dr. Don Dick
Chairman
Communications Department
Southern Missionary College
Collegedale, Tennessee 37315

## Tennessee, University of

Dr. Darrel W. Holt
Department of Broadcasting
College of Communications
University of Tennessee
Knoxville, Tennessee 37916

## TEXAS

## Baylor University

Dr. Peter Pringle
Director
Division of Radio-TV-Film
Baylor University
Waco, Texas 76703

## **East Texas State University

Station Manager
KETR
East Texas Station
East Texas State University
Commerce, Texas 75428

## Houston, University of

Dr. William Hawes
Department of Communications
University of Houston
Houston, Texas 77004

## **Lamar University

Jerry C. Hudson
Director
Radio/Television
Lamar University
Box 10050
Beaumont, Texas 77710

## **Navarro College

Barbara J. Lacy
Director of Television
Dept. of Radio-TV
Navarro College
West Hwy. 31—P. O. Box 1170
Corsicana, Texas 75110

## North Texas State University

Dr. Edwin Glick
Division of Radio-TV-Film
North Texas State University
Denton, Texas 76203

## Sam Houston State University

Dr. Robert Eubanks
Director of Broadcasting
Radio-TV-Film
Department of Speech & Drama
Sam Houston State University
Huntsville, Texas 77340

**\*\*San Antonio College**

Prof. Jean M. Longwith
Faculty Director of Broadcasting
Department of Speech & Drama
San Antonio College
1300 San Pedro Avenue
San Antonio, Texas 78212

**Southern Methodist University**

Dr. J. B. McGrath, Jr.
Chairman
Department of Broadcast-Film Art
Southern Methodist University
Dallas, Texas 75222

**Stephen F. Austin State University**

Dr. William J. Oliver
Department of Communication
Stephen F. Austin State University
Box 3048, SFA Station
Nacogdoches, Texas 75962

**\*\*Texas A&I University**

Prof. Gary Brooks
Department of Speech & Drama
Campus Box 215
Texas A&I University
Kingsville, Texas 78363

**Texas Christian University**

Dr. R. C. Norris
Head
Division of Radio-TV-Film
Department of Speech
Texas Christian University
Fort Worth, Texas 76129

**Texas Tech University**

Prof. Clive J. Kinghorn
Dept. of Mass Communications
P. O. Box 4080
Texas Tech University
Lubbock, Texas 79409

**Texas, University of—Arlington**

Dr. J. S. Gibson
Dept. of Communication
The University of Texas at Arlington
P. O. Box 19107
Arlington, Texas 76019

**Texas, University of—Austin**

Dr. Robert E. Davis
Chairman
Dept. of Radio-TV-Film
University of Texas
Austin, Texas 78712

**\*\*Texas Woman's University**

Prof. Thornton A. Klos
Department of Speech
Texas Woman's University
Box 3775, TWU Station
Denton, Texas 76204

**Trinity University**

Dr. Bill Hays, Chairman
Dept. of Journalism, Broadcasting & Film
Communications Film
715 Stadium Drive
Trinity University
San Antonio, Texas 78284

**UTAH**

**Brigham Young University**

Dr. Owen S. Rich
Department of Communication
E509 Harris Fine Arts Center
Brigham Young University
Provo, Utah 84601

**Utah State University**

Dr. Burrell Hansen
Director
Radio-TV
Department of Communication

Utah State University, UMC 07
Logan, Utah 84322

**Utah, University of**

Dr. Robert K. Tiemens
Director
Division of Journalism & Mass
  Communications
University of Utah
Salt Lake City, Utah 84112

**VERMONT**

**\*\*Vermont, University of**

Prof. William Lewis
Dept. of Speech & Drama
University of Vermont
Pomeroy Hall
Burlington, Vermont 05401

**VIRGINIA**

**James Madison University**

Dr. Charles Turner
Director of Radio-TV-Film
Dept. of Communications
James Madison University
Harrisonburg, Virginia 22801

**Norfolk State College**

Director, Mass CMU
Box 2300
Dept. of Mass Communication
Norfolk State College
2401 Corprew Avenue
Norfolk, Virginia 23504

**\*\*Washington & Lee University**

Prof. R. H. MacDonald
Department of Journalism
Washington & Lee University
Lexington, Virginia 24450

**WASHINGTON**

**\*\*Central Washington State College**

Prof. Roger R. Reynolds
Director of Broadcasting
Dept. of Mass Media
Central Washington State College
Ellensburg, Washington 98926

**\*\*Walla Walla College**

Loren Dickinson
General Manager
KGTS-FM
Walla Walla College
College Place, Washington
  99324

**Washington State University**

Prof. Val E. Limburg
Department of Communications
Washington State University
Pullman, Washington 99163

**Washington, University of**

Prof. Pat Cranston
Radio-TV Department DS-40
School of Communications
Room 133, CMU
University of Washington
Seattle, Washington 98195

**WEST VIRGINIA**

**Marshall University**

Dr. Dorothy R. Johnson
Chairman
Department of Speech
Marshall University
Huntington, West Virginia 25701

**West Virginia University**

Broadcast Journalism Sequence
School of Journalism
West Virginia University
Morgantown, West Virginia
  26506

## WISCONSIN

### **Beloit College

Prof. Carl G. Balson
Department of Speech
Beloit College
Beloit, Wisconsin 53511

### Marquette University

Dean Alfred J. Sokolnicki
College of Speech
Marquette University
Milwaukee, Wisconsin 53233

### **University of Wisconsin—Eau Claire

Dr. Robert L. Bailey
Chairman
Radio-TV-Film Area
University of Wisconsin
Eau Claire, Wisconsin 54701

### University of Wisconsin—Madison

Dr. Joanne Cantor
Dept. of Communication Arts
University of Wisconsin
Vilas Hall
821 University Avenue
Madison, Wisconsin 53706

### **University of Wisconsin—Oshkosh

Dr. Robert L. Snyder
Department of Speech
University of Wisconsin
Oshkosh, Wisconsin 54901

### **University of Wisconsin—Parkside

Dr. Alan M. Rubin
Communication Discipline
University of Wisconsin
Kenosha, Wisconsin 53141

### University of Wisconsin—Platteville

Dr. George Smith
University of Wisconsin-Platteville
College of Business, Industry and Communications
Platteville, Wisconsin 53818

### **University of Wisconsin—River Falls

Prof. Lorin Robinson
Chairman
Department of Journalism
Univ. of Wisconsin-River Falls
B-J 61582
River Falls, Wisconsin 54022

### **University of Wisconsin—Stevens Point

Dr. Robert J. Burull
University of Broadcasting
University of Wisconsin
Stevens Point, Wisconsin 54481

### **University of Wisconsin—Whitewater

Robert Leffingwell
Director of Radio
University of Wisconsin
Whitewater, Wisconsin 53190

## WYOMING

### **Central Wyoming College

Chairman
Radio-TV Broadcast
Central Wyoming College
Riverton, Wyoming 82501

### *Wyoming, University of

Department of Communication
University of Wyoming
Box 3314, University Station
Laramie, Wyoming 82701

## ABOUT THE CO-AUTHOR

Hal Bock has been a sportswriter for Associated Press since 1963. He has covered a wide range of sports and his assignments have taken him to the World Series, Super Bowl, the Olympics, and Stanley Cup playoffs.

He wrote DYNAMITE ON ICE: THE BOBBY ORR STORY, and SAVE! HOCKEY'S BRAVE GOALIES; he co-authored (with Rod Gilbert) GOAL! MY LIFE ON ICE, and (with Bill Chadwick) THE BIG WHISTLE, and was co-editor (with Zander Hollander) of THE COMPLETE ENCYCLOPEDIA OF ICE HOCKEY.